The
Telling Distance

Drawings by Johnson Charley

THE TELLING DISTANCE

Conversations with the American Desert

Bruce Berger

BREITENBUSH BOOKS, INC.

The author and publisher wish to express special appreciation to the Western States Arts Federation and its corporate and public sponsors.

The Western States Book Awards are a project of the Western States Arts Federation. The awards are supported by corporate founders The Xerox Foundation, the Lannan Foundation, Crane Duplicating Service, and the Witter Bynner Foundation for Poetry. Additional funding is provided by the National Endowment for the Arts Literature Program.

Breitenbush Books, Inc., P.O. Box 82157, Portland, Oregon 97282
James Anderson, publisher; Patrick Ames, editor in chief;
David Shetzline, editor in charge; Ky Krauthamer, designer

Breitenbush Books are distributed by Taylor Publishing Co., Dallas, Texas

First edition. 1 2 3 4 5 6 7 8 9
Manufactured in the United States of America

Library of Congress cataloging-in-publication data:
Berger, Bruce.
    The telling distance : conversations with the American desert /
Bruce Berger. — 1st ed.
    ISBN 0-932576-74-5
    1. Southwest, New—Description and travel—1981– 2. Desert ecology—
Southwest, New. 3. Berger, Bruce—Journeys—Southwest, New. I. Title.
F787.B47 1989
917.904'33—dc20   89–33144 CIP

Some of these pieces have appeared in the following publications: *Adventure Travel, Amelia, Aspen Magazine, Ceramics Monthly, Mountain Gazette, The New York Times, Not Man Apart, Outside, Rocky Mountain Magazine, Sonora Review, Southwest Review, Westways,* and *Wild America.*

"Genius of the Canyons," "Birdwatching: An Initiation," "Books on My Back," "Cold Pastoral," and "Science, Environmentalism, and Music" first appeared in *The North American Review.*

"Among My Souvenirs," which won the *Sierra* Nature Writing Contest, 1988, and "The Fire Sermon" first appeared in *Sierra.*

"The Mysterious Brotherhood" won the Ralph Kreiser Nonfiction Award, *Amelia,* 1986.

Excerpts from Everett Ruess's letters from *Everett Ruess: A Vagabond for Beauty* by W. L. Rusho (Gibbs Smith, Publisher: Layton, Utah); copyright © 1983 by Gibbs Smith. Used by permission.

◆   ◆

Contents

◆   ◆

Designer Deserts

Pinions, Piñons, and Opinions

Pursuit and Flight

◆   ◆

The Uses of Emptiness

◆   ◆

Introduction

The literature of the desert attempts a strange alchemy, one that tries to bring emptiness to a focus. Deserts are defined, after all, by their absence of life-giving water. That emptiness may launch the eye over expanses of dry arroyos, to snag it on a barbed horizon. More intimately, emptiness gapes between plants exiled by thirst, defending their claim to water, turning crumbled rock to life. A more dynamic emptiness is created by the person who walks down an arroyo scattering lizards, launching jackrabbits, exploding quail like grenades, sending doves squeaking skyward, leaving freshly abandoned sand. Drawing words to the vanishing point, speech about the desert is, quite literally, much ado about nothing.

Those possessed by that emptiness, however, will not keep silent. The desert notoriously harbors the loner, the misfit, the only child. They are downwardly mobile, and with such glamorous totems as the mountain lion and the bighorn sheep to pick from, they call themselves rats—desert rats. For all their urge to secede from their kind, they remain human beings—social animals—gifted with human tongues. Like Biblical prophets who repaired to the desert for visions to inflict on society, the modern desert pilgrim, less flammably, visits extremities and bears witness. The literature of the American wilderness, and particularly the desert, is full of exhibitionist hermits. But the witness, whatever his personal temptations, will ultimately be trying to bring back some testimony of the nonself, the deliverance of space, the refreshment of the waterless.

Given, then, that the notion of turning the waste into words is as absurd as any other volunteer activity, the question remains, how to make it happen? Clearly one cannot write about absence directly: one would trail into mystic blather, finally to repeat the same lame syllable. The only recourse is to write about absence indirectly, by invoking its exceptions. Like the hiker, the writer will gravitate to the oasis. He will wind up describing old lakebeds, cactus, the pronghorn, the owl. He will people the waste with fellow travelers, human or otherwise.

And being a social animal, he will record man's endless conversation with the desert in his arts, his fabrications, in the distortions of memory. He will observe desert companions divorced from the contexts that make sense of their follies. Because those follies endure, even in the desert, man and his civilization will gain a certain wry perspective. One of the desert's finer by-products is its dry wit.

And in that clear light, those who consider the desert will have to confront, finally, not just the friendly images of man's art and his irony, but his impact as meddler and destroyer. It is not just a matter of the cities, the extractive industries, the killing particulates, the dried riverbeds and mined aquifers, the war games and the sprawl. Those civilized activities are indeed overcoming the wastes we turn to for relief; timelessness is being wiped out by the moment. But beneath all of this, unsounded, is a shift in attitude that originates well beyond the desert it affects.

This shift was brought home to me by a piece of sculpture I recently saw at an art show in Phoenix. Sculpture is perhaps a loose term for twelve cubic feet of granite that have been shattered, then strung back together with pitons and wire. As a work of art its ugliness was merely fashionable, but as an icon it was clear. Whatever the artist intended, here was the perfect expression of a view of nature that has become widespread in popular belief, is quite new to human thought, and almost unexamined as a wellspring for human behavior. I stood among the contrivances in the museum, letting the image sink in, then bent to the title to see if the sculptor had left a clue to his intent. The piece was by John Young, of Denver, and is called "The Last Planet."

Until recently, whether nature was treated as something to be curbed or admired, it was seen as the repository of such emotions as wonder, terror, inspiration, reverence, dread, all that can be summed up by the single outmoded syllable: awe. The desert's specialized contribution took the form of heat, snakes, and the terrible absence of water—an absence notorious on a stretch like the Camino del Diablo along the southern border of Arizona, where hundreds died during the westward migration, and where, even now, the northern migration of Latin American job seekers is leaving its trail of cadavers next to plastic water jugs that proved insufficient. The view of nature as final arbiter ended with an experiment in the desert, followed by the bombs over Hiroshima and Nagasaki. Another possibility was born. Beyond the immediate horror, one learned that a few pounds of inorganic matter, released, could annihilate populations and render vast areas uninhabitable. Clearly a reasonable multiple of the same substance could erase all of life. For the first time nature the fearsome, throne of the gods, cave of demons, source of catastrophe and womb of the future, was shown to be mortal, vulnerable to human hands.

It has been widely noted that the roles on our planet are now reversed: man seems now the sustainer and destroyer, nature the mute supplicant. What has been less noticed is that the two most prominent views of nature— as life-giver and as threat—both emanated from a view of nature as power. Ours is the first generation to see nature as fragility—fragility summed up by a single image, the photograph of our planet from space. There, in an eyespan, is all of life we know. Biologist Lewis Thomas sees earth as a single cell—a cell that does not, to our knowledge, replicate. Alone against the blackness of an empty, expanding, entropic universe spins our tiny round home, a kind of celestial Fabergé egg. It is doubtful whether it is the kind of egg we can blast apart, then sling back together with pins and wire.

The desert rat caught up in this new awareness realizes that his desert—barbed, hot, hostile—too is fragile. At the very time that mining companies are gouging, developers are bulldozing, subsidized cows are devouring, and recreation vehicles are mashing and compacting our arid lands, often without a second thought, the sensitized foot traveler even worries about his own minor impact. Can he still afford to build a campfire, or must he spare the last dead wood and carry a butane burner? Can he trust the rat pack with his secret places? Should he invite hordes of fellow travelers so that they will apply the political pressures necessary to save these wastes from commercial ravage? Or will sensitive hordes trample these places themselves?

Today's desert traveler must pick his way between the immensity and the fragility. For many of us the refreshment of the waterless has become a necessity, whatever the warring concepts about our impact. Accepting the fact of our flesh, bringing down our boots with care, we can still, if briefly, give predictability the slip. For to walk into the desert is to deal one's life a wild card. The playing of that card allows the traveler to play his own individuality among the elemental forces. And just to have that card to play is to know that the game, however stacked, is not lost. To steep in silence, to absorb the long view, is to become more comfortable with the emptiness that surrounds us, even in civilization. Existence itself clarifies, with life and nonlife so starkly juxtaposed. Companioned by thoughts, associations, sensitivities, thick skin, protective coloration, and perhaps the right companions, the individual becomes

Bruce Berger

the very citizen of emptiness. The wanderer may find that he is, in fact, the oasis he seeks. The exile becomes the exile in residence.

No subject matter more closely exemplifies Eliot's phrase about language being "a raid on the inarticulate." Those who chase this land with words must thread their way through all the overlays—of harshness, humor, romance, vulnerability, and joy—that the desert invents in the human mind. Behind those mirages lie the actual spines and rocks one needs to reach, and sometimes it seems as if this bristling landscape so resists being written about that it will actively pursue the writer to his lair, to turn his weapons against him. As if to show me I wasn't merely being paranoid, the desert went so far as to issue a little parable on a night when, struggling with a particularly stubborn bit of description at a kitchen counter in Phoenix, my eye was caught by a scorpion scuttling across the linoleum. I grabbed the nearest heavy object, a thesaurus, dove from the stool, and shoved the book wildly along the floor so as to mash the scorpion against the refrigerator. The scorpion's revenge was that the stopped book caught my little finger, almost bending it backward in imitation of its tail's graceful curve. It was as if the desert, with its usual dry wit, were throwing the book at me.

From emptiness to speech—armed with that brick of words—a chasm must be leapt. But the more telling distance lies between creatures themselves. Here are a few of their tales.

WILD INTERIORS

JOHNSON CHARLEY

Genius of the Canyons

To imagine desperate adventures in extravagant locales is a right of adolescence. But to abandon your comfortable home, buy the mules and supplies, find the adventures fulfilling beyond your wildest conception, snag it in words and paints, then disappear before your twenty-first birthday, requires a kind of genius. And Everett Ruess has become a genius in the older, rarer sense of *inhabiting spirit:* a genius of place.

Even today the expanses of the Colorado Plateau are impressive. Vast emptiness, extending from Southeast Utah and Northern Arizona into New Mexico and Colorado, reaches toward sculpted horizons, through which even today's motorist crawls like a molecule through a sand painting. Life, represented by bursts of green, scattered towns and wandering animals, is doubly precious for its contrast to rock, sand and sky: all that life is not. And the very flatness is deceptive, dropping into gashes hundreds of feet deep, or into separate, partially habitable worlds. The basic unit of any desert is the grain of sand, and on the Colorado Plateau the grain of sand is red. Vermilion, rust, ruby, cayenne: they are all here, colored by the very iron that colors our blood. Such country almost resists life, but once you have let it into your system, it strangely persists.

When Everett Ruess first reached the Colorado Plateau in 1931, at the age of eighteen, its margins were threaded by eccentric dirt roads and the only firm crossing was forged across Northern Arizona by the Santa Fe Railroad

The
Telling
Distance

and Route 66. The earlier population seemed so remote that the Navajos referred to them as the Anasazi, or "someone's ancestors." Six hundred years earlier the Anasazi had abandoned the narrow canyons that spread from the Colorado River, doubtless because of drought, and found lusher havens in Arizona and New Mexico. Small ranching communities sprang up during the period of Mormon colonization in the late nineteenth century, ringing the canyon country, and a few Anglo traders invaded the Navajos to the south. Between these far settlements, particularly among the canyons radiating from the Colorado River, lay the most compelling American desolation south of Alaska.

From the beginning Everett showed a parallel interest in adventure and the arts. As a small child he experimented with sketching, clay-modeling and woodcarving. He began keeping a literary journal at twelve, and first tasted the wilds on a scout camping trip at thirteen. His concept of adventure was romantic in the extreme, and in late adolescence he confided to his journal, "One night, long ago, while I tossed restlessly upon my bed, an idea crystallized within me . . . I lay suddenly still, taut, and filled with a tremendous superabundance of energy that demanded outlet. My brain was busied with tense imaginings of adventures in far places . . . Bitter pain is in store for me, but I shall bear it. Beauty beyond all power to convey shall be mine; I will search diligently for it. Death may await me; with vitality, impetuosity and confidence I will combat it. Not through cynicism and ennui will I be easy prey. And regardless of all that may befall, let me not be found to lack an understanding of the inscrutable humor of it all . . ." Such stylistic deep purple, full not only of the call of adventure but admiration for the stoic adventurer, seems almost a projection of Kipling's "If." The passage is saved from Victorian simplicity only by the fact that, in Ruess's case, it all happened to be true.

In flight from the constriction of cities, Everett was in

no way in flight from his own home. Extensive letters to family and friends, published after his disappearance, reflect that his parents supported him emotionally and, to a lesser degree, financially, and did not pester him for news even when he kept them in constant anxiety for his safety. His mother produced booklets of block prints, wrote verse, taught Everett artistic techniques and held poetry readings in the house. His father held two degrees from Harvard, worked briefly as a Unitarian pastor, was Director of Education and Research at the Los Angeles County Probation Department, and was involved in the problems of the aging. And Everett's older brother Waldo worked in the California deserts for the Metropolitan Water District of Los Angeles at the very time that Everett wandered alone further east. To Waldo he wrote with a warmth not above criticism, remarking, "You are probably enjoying life anyhow, even though you do not live it to the full," and "Don't leave your problems to be solved by Time—the solution might be adverse"—as if he were the older brother.

Everett treated time as the enemy, and despite the slowness of burros he covered an impressive amount of terrain. In four years he ranged as far east as Gallup and Shiprock, New Mexico, explored Mesa Verde in Colorado, dropped into the Sonoran Desert thinking the cactus forest would provide good subjects for watercolors, wandered the Navajo Reservation, reached the bottom of the Grand Canyon, and at last returned to the Utah canyon country, his favorite. It was common for him to travel thirty-five miles in a day, and once he wrote that "I have wandered over more than 400 miles with the burros, these last six weeks, paying no attention to trails, except as they happened to serve me, and finding my water as I went. I never went two days without discovering it."

Such migrations would seem a recipe for loneliness. Only rarely did Everett have company, and only for short stretches, yet he was not shy or antisocial. He stayed at a

The Telling Distance

ranch long enough to learn to wrangle, and paused several weeks with an archeological expedition in Monument Valley, absorbing all he could while terrifying archeologists with his fearlessness about heights. In Escalante, Utah, he rode horseback and hunted for arrowheads with the Mormon boys, then took them to the movies, and from Flagstaff, Arizona, he wrote, "I met a couple of wandering Navajos, and we stayed up most of the night talking, eating roast mutton with black coffee, and singing songs. The songs of the Navajo express for me something that no other songs do." It was the Indians who most fascinated him, and their hospitality flowered when he learned to speak Navajo. He was invited to pray with a medicine man over a sick Navajo child, and was the only Anglo allowed to participate in the Hopi antelope dance. "I know the Indians now," he writes, "have lived with them and exchanged gifts, and enjoyed the hospitality of the finest of them, riding their horses and taking part in their ceremonies. I know the white people too—all the traders in this locality, and strange experiences I have had with them, but I like the Indians better. I had two friends among the whites, but one was driven from the country by misfortune, and the other was killed a week ago. A truck lost a wheel and the load fell and crushed him."

But he wrote more tellingly from the town where he took the boys to the movies, "It is true that I miss intelligent companionship, but there are so few with whom I can share the things that mean much to me that I have learned to contain myself." Later he explained more fully, "It is not that I am unable to enjoy companionship or unable to adapt myself to other people. But I dislike to bring into play the aggressiveness of spirit which is necessary with an assertive companion, and I have found it easier and more adventurous to face situations alone. There is a splendid freedom in solitude . . . nothing stands between me and the wild." It is significant that beneath the youthful fervor is mature knowledge of the limits of sharing, and the need for inner self-sufficiency. Humanity is one strand of his adventure, not to be given unwarranted stress.

And he had much besides people to sustain him. He was seldom without the company of three animals, including successive pairs of burros, occasionally horses, that served as pack animals. While burros are not stimulating company and often made him impatient, he found they redeemed themselves when they stood up to their knees in wildflowers, blossoms on their lips, staring at him with lustrous brown eyes. There was probably more companionship with the mongrel Curly, whom he acquired outside Kayenta one night when he heard a squealing for help, stroked the source's fur, and sparks flew into the dark.

But Ruess's chief companion was a fervent imagination, fired by books his parents relayed to him at mail stops. From Superior, Arizona, he wrote that he was sending back *Candide,* which he enjoyed, *The Satyricon,* which he found interesting but unimportant, and works by Balzac and Dunsany. He was keeping *The Brothers Karamazov,* and asked them to send novels by Walpole and Dos Passos, Mann's *The Magic Mountain,* and *The Anthology of Modern Poetry.* He also wanted his copy of Havelock Ellis's *The Dance of Life,* the book he claimed most influenced him, and which he wanted to reread. His first burros were named Pegasus and Perry (for Pericles), and a later horse was called Nuflo after a character in *Green Mansions:* he seemed to live in a kind of literary democracy. His passionate reading probably helped resign his parents to his lack of formal education, and served to infuse his experience with a mythic resonance. Of his painting he spoke less, noting with satisfaction when he sold watercolors for supply money, and sending a package to his parents explaining that several were failures to be reworked later, and apologizing for spots in the sky occasioned by frost in the paint.

Ruess besieged the Colorado Plateau in a continuing

dream that included rattlesnakes, scorpions, black widows, quicksand, flash floods, treacherous ledges, illness, drought. "A scorpion started to crawl into my blankets, but I stopped him in time," he wrote from Flagstaff. "I killed my eighth rattler of the summer—a rare species found only in the Grand Canyon." From Canyon de Chelly he wrote, "I very narrowly escaped being gored to death by a wild bull, and there was a harrowing sequel when he discovered my camp that night, somewhile between midnight and dawn." From Kayenta: "Yesterday morning I found a big centipede in my pack. When I walked to Rainbow bridge at dawn I found a six-inch scorpion beside my bed at dawn." And from Zion: "For six days I've been suffering from my semi-annual poison ivy— my sufferings are far from over. For two days I couldn't tell whether I was dead or alive. I writhed and twisted in the heat, with swarms of ants and flies crawling over me, while the poison oozed and crusted on my face and arms and back. I ate nothing—there was nothing to do but suffer philosophically."

Bruce Berger

The tribulations were less philosophical for his pack animals. Pericles and Pegasus proved too old and weak, requiring Everett to haul part of the load himself, so he sold them and bought others in Superior, Arizona, saving five of the twenty dollars his parents sent for the purpose. His burros bolted with all his equipment outside Kayenta, but mercifully turned up in the night. In the well-named Canyon del Muerto, a pack horse fell off the trail and was killed. Dark was fast descending and Everett reached a dry cave. "The skies were murky and I had not eaten since morning, so I fried some mutton and sweet bread. Then I read Browning and pondered."

Height was probably the greatest danger faced by man and burro, particularly the cliffs Everett risked to get to promising ruins. Climbers usually favor the right side or the left, a phenomenon Everett discovered in Mesa Verde when he reached a ruin by working across a ledge six to eighteen inches wide, only to return backward on his knees. An archeologist Ruess helped later wrote, "One time in camp he stood on the edge of a 400 foot cliff during a rainstorm and did a water-color sketch of a waterfall. I remember this very clearly because I was scared to death just watching him perched on the edge of the cliff." Ruess himself admitted the danger, but put the risk in perspective. "Vijalmar Stefanson, the Arctic explorer, says that adventures are a sign of unpreparedness and incompetence. I think he is largely right, nevertheless I like adventure and enjoy taking chances when skill and fortitude play a part. If we never had any adventures, we would never know what stuff was in us."

What clearly carried Ruess through solitude and adversity, more than literature, art or a sense of his own romance, was sheer relish for all he encountered. Visions waited in ambush—double rainbows, the "sheer incurving cliffs, breathlessly chiseled and gloriously colored," the "lunatic quiver of a coyote," the "whiplashes of rain." He would sit in an abandoned Navajo hogan, watching the circle of light from the sky-hole shift over matted leaves from hour to hour. Scornful of jewelry, he spent his last money on a turquoise bracelet because "It is like having a bit of sky on my wrist." Storms didn't mean discomfort but the drama of darkness, wind and rain. He plunged through all with his senses alert, singing favorite melodies from Brahms and Dvorak. Experience was not divided between the good and the ill, but between the intense and the less intense.

And through the exuberance of his prose he made his values clear, to the point of being cutting. To a writer he met, he wrote, "Personally I have no least desire for fame. I feel only a stir of distaste when I think of being called 'the well known author' or 'the great artist.' I have no desire to bend my efforts toward entertaining the bored and blasé world. And that's what writing amounts to—or at least, your kind, I think. It would help to occupy a few hours . . .

Then, more thoroughly satisfied with their own more peaceful or otherwise superior lives, they would use the magazines to start a fire or sell to the junk man." This seeming cruelty prefaced a letter meant to startle the recipient into experiencing more deeply. He knew that joy was his own creation. "I feel much freer than I did in the city, but that is due not only to a change in environment, but to a change in my mental attitude." He says he has "constantly known beauty so piercing as to be almost unbearable," but has been able to scorn worlds he has enjoyed "like half-burnt candles." "Finality doesn't appall me, and I seem always to enjoy things the more intensely because of the certainty they will not last . . . The things I've loved and given up without a complaint have returned to me doubled." With the sense of one of those desert creatures conjured out of nothing, he writes, "I never cease to wonder at the impossibility that I live. Even when to my senses the world is not incredibly beautiful or fantastic, I am overwhelmed by the appalling strangeness and intricacy of the curiously tangled knot of life, and at the way that knot unwinds, making everything clear and inevitable . . ." And, "To live is to be happy; to be carefree, to be overwhelmed by the glory of it all." Ruess may have been bolstered by his readings of Havelock Ellis and others, but literary dances so sorely put to the test can only have struck resonance in a born ecstatic.

Yet along with joy approaching self-oblivion came an increasing carelessness. In his last year he remarked, "This time in my wanderings I have had more reckless self-confidence than ever before . . . Hundreds of times I have trusted my life to crumbling sandstone or nearly vertical angles in search for water or cliff dwellings." Phrases ring like a premonition. "The picturesque gear of packing, and my gorgeous Navajo saddle blankets, make a place my own. But when I go I leave no trace . . ." and "I feel more detached from life, somehow gentler . . . Meanwhile I have used my body mercilessly, seldom giving way to it

Bruce Berger

until forced, so that I should not wonder if it will turn traitor to me sometime. Anyway as Omar says, 'If the soul can naked on the air of heaven ride, were't not a shame for him in this clay carcass crippled to abide?' That is a big 'if' but may the time never come when I have to minister to my body." And describing the view northwest from the top of Navajo Mountain, he wrote to his parents, "the country between here and the San Juan and Colorado rivers and beyond them is as rough and impenetrable a territory as I have ever seen. Thousands of domes and towers of sandstone lift their rounded pink tops from the blue and purple shadows. To the east, great canyons seam the desert, cutting vermilion gashes through the grey green of the sage-topped mesas." He was gazing directly into the labyrinth where, half a year later, he would vanish.

The Escalante country today includes the most spec-tacular of surviving canyons, yet the river itself, gouging the dramatic system, is peaceful, almost sleepy. Banks of willows toss in waves like grain, with here and there a Russian olive brushed silver by the wind, sprouting from seeds washed down from the town of Escalante. Milk-weeds and cattails suggest the rural Midwest, and in the fall, when Everett set off, the leaves of cottonwood and willow, the flowers of clover, sunflower, snakeweed and rabbit brush turn degrees of yellow, into which miniature asters burn blue as sea caves. Overhead stretch calm laterals of sandstone, copper, sienna and peach, which the river bleeds with sky in eddies and swirls. Slants of sun bring the walls into relief, finding them pitted and knobbed, pocked, stippled and gouged, cross-hatched like an ele-phant, scored like a pineapple. Animals flash and are gone, but one can study the prints of mountain lion and deer wound through the sand, perhaps by chance, perhaps in a motif of pursuit and flight like the figures on Keats' urn. Flickers in pairs peak and swoop, peak and swoop, flashing salmon, and at evening the insect eaters appear over the cliffs, bats flitting irrationally, swifts in backtracking darts:

animals and birds after the same prey.

In the half-world of side canyons, that chaos of domes and towers, blue and purple shadows that struck Everett from Navajo Mountain, light leaks down the sheer naves of walls, reflecting back and forth until the canyon attains a directionless radiance: a microworld suspended in amber. Here one trades the horizontal for the vertical, the expansive for the intimate. Footsteps crunch on cool pink sand. Pale flowers of the night-bloomers, the great star of the evening primrose, the trumpet of the jimson weed, remain open all day, and a single box elder may bask in a shaft of light, curly as endive and impossibly green. Walls are streaked with minerals washed over the rim, and a hollowed seep may be laterally fringed with monkey flower, columbine, maidenhair fern and a small orchid known as helleborine, an alcove delicate as a Pompeian frieze. In such stillness an insect is a major intruder and a dropped hat reports like a sonic boom. For the hiker the canyon may end in a blackened shaft over a pool, only to continue hundreds of feet overhead, accessible to birds and lizards, back into the imagination.

It was into such country that Everett headed with two burros from the town of Escalante in mid-November, 1934. To his brother he wrote, "As to when I shall visit civilization, it will not be soon," and to his parents, "I am going toward the river now, through some rather wild country . . . So I might not have a post office for a couple of months. I am taking an ample supply of food with me . . . As I have more money than I need now, I am sending you $10, and I want each of you to spend five for something you have been wishing to have—books, or a trip, but not anything connected with any kind of duty."

Knowing that Everett did not like to be pressed for his whereabouts, his parents waited nearly three months before they wrote to the postmistress of Escalante asking for any report of him. When none was forthcoming, they wrote to the post offices of all the other towns from which

Bruce Berger

he had sent mail, to county sheriffs, newspapers, radio stations, forest rangers, Indian agents—anyone they could think of. *The Los Angeles Evening Herald* broke the news, and from then on the story was national drama. The only comfort the Ruesses received was reassurance that Everett could handle himself in the wilderness.

In early March a dozen men from the town of Escalante set off to search the Escalante River system. In Davis Gulch, a side canyon near the Escalante's confluence with the Colorado, they found the two burros starving but still alive in a cul-de-sac that Everett had barricaded, as well as Everett's boots and a handful of sherds he had collected. In a cave nearby they found the inscription "Nemo 1934" carved in Everett's hand on the doorway of an Anasazi ruin. Meanwhile, a placer miner from Hanksville, Utah, visited the Ruesses in their home and proposed hiring Navajo trackers. The Ruesses subsidized his expedition, but nothing came of it.

In early June the Associated Civic Clubs of Southern Utah, representing fifteen counties, dispatched another dozen men on a lengthier, better organized search of the terrain around Davis Gulch. They met two sheepmen who said Ruess had camped a couple of nights with them in late November, and that Everett had refused a gift of some mutton, preferring to travel light. They also turned up a second Nemo inscription by some Anasazi pictographs.

The inscriptions are doubly baffling in that Everett disapproved of scarring the wilderness, and Nemo, in Latin, means "no one." The name was meaningless to the searchers, who wired an inquiry to Everett's parents. Mrs. Ruess wired back that one of the books Everett read in the desert was the T. E. Lawrence translation of *The Odyssey*, and that Odysseus was "no one" in Greek. Odysseus saved himself from the one-eyed giant Polyphemus, she said, by the trick of calling himself Nemo. She was mistaken in that "Outis," or "no one," is the name Odysseus gave to Polyphemus. Everett's father later decided that Everett was more likely thinking of another of his favorite books, Jules Verne's *Twenty Thousand Leagues Under the Sea.* Everett may have identified with the book's Captain Nemo, who hated civilization, explored unknown lands in the ocean, and invented a new language—just as Everett was exploring unknown deserts and learning the new language of Navajo.

Later that June the Ruesses made a fruitless 2,400 mile trip to all the places Everett had been, and meanwhile national publicity had generated the predictable response. An unidentified corpse was found near Gallup, New Mexico, but dental evidence proved it could not be Everett. The reporter who cracked the Leopold and Loeb case by finding Leopold's spectacles was rushed in to no avail. Psychics across the country revealed that Everett was living among the Navajos, that he had drowned, and couldn't agree whether he was dead or alive. Tourists reported encounters with mysterious young strangers who could only be Everett. And his parents dreamed that he simply showed up at the back door, saying, "Well, here I am." In May of 1964, thirty years later, as the area was being drowned by Lake Powell, Everett's brother Waldo made one more search with professional guides, and found nothing.

Bruce Berger

There are numerous conjectures, all contradicted by one detail. Cattle rustlers were known to pass through the area, and false rumors were deliberately circulated that FBI agents were on their trail. It is conceivable that they killed Everett for his supplies, or because they suspected he was an agent—yet in an area where footprints last up to two years under the overhangs, the finest Navajo trackers found plenty of Everett's own tracks, and none of anyone else's. It is possible, given his increasing recklessness, that Everett fell off a ledge into a crevice that hid his remains, but he would have had to fall with all his gear except his boots. It is possible that he drowned trying to cross the Colorado with his equipment on an improvised raft—but it was not in his character to leave two animals to starve. And it is possible that he really intended to become Nemo, no one, to vanish into another identity and leave Everett behind: but again he would have to abandon the burros, not to mention the family and friends to whom he was fiercely loyal (it is a credit to his family's generosity that his father has written, "Even if he were found alive, we would have no desire to interfere with his fulfillment of his life and destiny").

Speculation remains fascinating, and fruitless in the absence of hard evidence. Among subsequent tributes, his parents used a small insurance policy on his life to sponsor the Everett Ruess Poetry Awards, open to young people in the Southwest. A selection of his letters ran serially in *Desert Magazine* in 1939, and a more complete selection was published by Desert Magazine Press in a book called *On Desert Trails with Everett Ruess*, together with a selection of poems, paintings, and block prints. More recently there has been a minor Ruess boom. Quotations from Ruess have appeared with increasing frequency on wilderness calendars, and the radical environmental group Earth First! has elevated Ruess into a cult figure. In 1983, Peregrine Smith Books brought out an expanded collection of letters and artwork, along with an account of Ruess's life by W. L. Rusho, under the title, *Everett Ruess: A Vagabond for Beauty*—amassing under one cover what remained of Everett Ruess.

But there was more. In 1985, Gibbs Smith, publisher of *A Vagabond for Beauty*, arranged a commemoration of Ruess in Davis Gulch, fifty years after he had left the last trace of himself in that spot. Among the invited were Waldo Ruess, Everett's older brother and the recipient of so many of the letters, and Clive Kincaid, founder of the Southern Utah Wilderness Alliance, which used a silhouette of Everett and his two burros as its logo. Conversation revealed that Clive Kincaid's mother lived just a half mile from Waldo Ruess's house in Santa Barbara, and Kincaid started calling on Waldo during family visits.

From surviving prints and old photographs Kincaid knew that there were Ruess prints for which the original blocks had disappeared, and he asked Waldo about them in the summer of 1986. Waldo remembered that back in the forties his children had played with some linoleum blocks of Everett's, using them as building blocks. They ransacked Waldo's attic and garage, then came upon them in the garden shed. Excitedly they spread them on the lawn. There were some fifteen of them, so worn and eaten by weather that Kincaid feared they would be useless for making new prints. Waldo recruited an artist friend, who spent two months with an assistant preparing them for a limited edition. More block prints were created from surviving prints. A premier showing at the Salt Lake City Public Library with Waldo in attendance drew a crowd of two hundred, and a set of the prints began a two-year tour of the state. Everett himself made no great claims for his art, sending it home with apologies or trading it for supplies. It is a curious extension of his legend that a half-century after his disappearance he has brought in $25,000 to help the Southern Utah Wilderness Alliance defend what's left of the country he treasured.

These recent publications and uncovered artworks give us an expanded look at Ruess the creator. The art shows grace, balance, and a keen eye for form—but little more—while the poetry, despite flashes, remains too ripe with grandeur to retain interest. A lyric called "Wilderness Song" bears enough resemblance to "The Great Lover" to suggest that Rupert Brooke may have been an influence. Ruess was, of course, out of touch with others creating at the same time, and he was certainly too unstoppably on the move to develop his arts in a methodical way. His most striking creations are the single phrases, finely observed, originally expressed, that still leap absolutely fresh from the lushest passages of the letters. His deep feelings, his intelligence, his singularity as a person, even his surprising taste as a reader, all suggest a power he hadn't reached. The way he tried every medium that came to hand indicates that he was still searching for a voice, a vehicle of expression, for feelings that simply overflowed. It is possible that once those feelings had found their most responsive forms, he would have become one of our great originals.

What he left us, then, was not great artwork or verse, but, in breathtakingly few years, a great life. Never was his example more crucial. The Colorado Plateau that Everett loved, still magnificent, is increasingly crossed and scarred by roads and bike trails, pitted with mines, stripped by cattle, deadened with fly ash, ravished by indifference. In the most tragic act of federal vandalism to befall the American West, Glen Canyon Dam drowned the very heart of the canyon country, the great Colorado system that Everett just reached when he disappeared. The reservoir allowed the Upper Basin states to lay claim to their share of the water by impounding it bodily rather than being given credit for it on paper, causing two hundred miles of America's most radiant canyons to silt up under the stilled water, speed boats, oil slicks and bobbing styrofoam cups of Lake Powell. Most of the Escalante system lies beyond the reservoir's reach, and retains in miniature what was lost under the lake. Yet it too, with its upper drainages, has been threatened by proposed roads, utility corridors, heavy timbering and the mining of carbon dioxide. Even now the lower end of the Escalante is lost under Lake Powell, and if the remains of Everett repose in Davis Gulch, they too, along with his notebook, his last paintings, his turquoise bracelet like a piece of the sky, are silting up forever.

Ruess was almost the first to travel that country not to prospect, to herd cattle, to scheme a railroad or escape from the law, but simply to relish it, to absorb it, and to shape that love in the arts. Many who have discovered the Escalante since feel a similar passion, and return as he did, like addicts, needing that country, feeling heartsick that it could be burned into mindless energy. What Everett bequeaths them is the sense of ecstatic seeking, of limitless adventure, of going where you will and leaving no trace. His very disappearance, as if into sandstone itself, arrests him in the extreme of his passion, his hunger for life, his unending youth. Ours is not an age of inhabiting spirits. But Ruess, whatever his fate, has entered our common memory, as mythic and as real as the canyons themselves. His life, like the stone, is a form of light, and his very mystery soars into permanent joy.

Bruce
Berger

Wild Interiors

It would be reassuring if those of us who haunt the canyon country today did so with the purity of an Everett Ruess: alone, ecstatic, stripped to essentials. But Ruess was an anomaly in his own time, and given the comparative accessibility of the deserts he traveled, advances in equipment, the very manner in which character is shaped, an unlikely figure like Everett may have become an impossibility. Even with lightweight gear that allows the traveler to become his own pack animal, lone adventurers are increasingly rare. Today most hardened desert rats run in a pack, plan ahead like accountants, and have honed their trips to rituals that may say more about themselves than the barrens through which they pass.

The Telling Distance

Most often an itinerary hatches in a single brain, biding its moment to seed the minds of others. Among my own friends two are map-mad, love to argue, and through capitulation or compromise a scheme develops. For the rest of us the planning phase is intolerable and we keep politely out of the way—to maximize the hand of chance or from laziness—and concentrate on the casting. Would love to take Norman if he didn't drag along Glad; Brian never shuts up but knows the waterholes. Here one needn't pore over maps to have an opinion, and it is critical to intrude. The classic number of participants is still one, but I once had a satisfying Wilderness Experience with a troop of eleven. Travel may be the most difficult activity one performs with others—and wilderness travel the most difficult sub-species—but it is comforting to remember that any well-planned trip has a healthy mortality rate, and that overpopulation often solves itself as the date approaches.

As deadly as the planning is the actual preparation. With pouches of turkey Tetrazzini, compressed peas that rehydrate into algae blooms, goose-down bedding and clothing, nylon shelter, aluminum frame baggage and campfires of compressed gas, one would think that technology had leeched the personality out of getting ready. Yet even here it may erupt. I have friends, for instance, who spend weeks mashing apricots, pears, bananas, plums and strawberries into a paste, which they dry in the sun and combine into shapes that resemble a set of UNESCO flags. They sew their favorite grind of coffee into porous sacks, stow each day's ration of junk food into form-fitting ziploc bags they make with a kit, divide the salami into numbered portions that double as a calendar. Each article of clothing is folded into a separate plastic bag and packed so meticulously that their retrieval system, if squeaky, is precise as a data bank; on the ninth day of mud they look as if they had stepped from a catalogue. Others in the same gang leave everything to the last afternoon, when the stores are down to chili and lasagna, and jam their packs like emergency Christmas stockings.

More telling than the way one packs for a trip is the way one packs against it. One will have to stay well enough to limp back to the car, or heal oneself, and a measure of self-assurance is the personal pharmacopoeia. It may start with just bandaids and disinfectant, escalate to cold tablets, ankle and knee supports, then maybe a snake bite kit, old Darvon, film cans of DMSO, an arsenal likely to swell as the push-off looms. More insidious are the placebos that get stashed in case one gets sick, held up by the weather or (one shrinks from the word) bored. Without months and mules at one's disposal, one can't afford the kind of portable library demanded by Everett Ruess. A fellow

Bruce
Berger

compulsive reader, new to camping, asked me what kind of book was best suited. Through experiment I have found that the optimum book is one you have always wanted to go back to: you are assured of welcome reading, but knowing how it comes out you will not become so engrossed as to miss the trip. *Any* book, objected a mutual friend, contaminates attention, divides the mind and is the mental equivalent of the junk food in his little ziplocs. Deciding we both had a point, the novice packed two paperback mysteries and a plastic bag full of snacks so copious it became known as the piñata.

The low point of any trip must be the outward drive and disposal of the cars, particularly if they are to be installed at either end. One may regret having kept out of the planning, for the mad Magellans are back at the helm. Let's see, if we put three people and four packs in the Wagoneer, four people and three packs in the Scout, two of each in the Toyota, leave the Toyota and the packs and seven people at the point of departure, drive the other two cars to the point of return, leave the Wagoneer and bring back the Scout . . . Getting a grip on it can exhaust a geometer, the actual execution over pitted back roads can devour a day, and you start to wonder just who dreamt this caper up. Nor is it comforting to remember that it must all be unraveled when you are stinking and ready for home.

But at last combustion is stilled and the cars, after several false starts, definitively locked. Ears ring with the stillness. Packs are shouldered, the first steps taken: it is the moment of free-fall before the parachute opens. What if I lose the car keys en route? Should I have hidden them outside the car, or would that have gotten it stolen? What if locals sabotage the tires? I wonder if that cumulus means a front moving in. Is that a twinge in my right knee? Did I pack the repellent and spare flashlight batteries I bought when we stopped for enchiladas?

It is staggering to realize that five years from now nearly every detail of the trip until this minute will have been lost. The life one leaves, with its sharp divisions between work and play, its competing realities of magazines, newspapers, movies and television, the threats from the Middle East or North Africa or the local reactor, its time sliced into hours and space into city blocks, fractures and refractures the living rhythm; like a painting by Braque or Picasso, our experience of the world is essentially cubist. Preparation and journey to the wilderness, with their anticipations, anxieties and practical considerations, partake of the same splintering, and it takes a while for the jangled senses to smooth themselves out. The miracle is that it happens.

After a few hours, or a few days, the new cycle takes over. It is resisted by those who carry watches wound to the minute, who can match every step with some squiggle on a map. But eventually real time becomes the sun's journey from one horizon to another, or a succession of those journeys, and distance is what the foot can achieve by time's light. Space, no longer a grid, expands into peaks and canyons or contracts when the going is smooth; time shrinks when rimrock or the seasons wall out the light, or swells with the cold and dark. Change, no longer a break in context, unfolds in lengths of shadow and refigured horizons, or wheels with the cycle of sun and stars. There are no receptors outside one's skin. As with primitive peoples or a particle in contemporary physics, time and space are an axis passing through oneself.

Because wilderness travelers tend to be loners who gather into groups, during the day they often string themselves out, letting their attention merge with the landscape or sink into themselves. A hypnotic alertness takes over; one's senses become a crossroads for rocks and mountains, sky and birds, and personality seeps into eclipse. Gathering, splitting and regrouping, a party of campers is a kind of solipsist society, a trail of contiguous solos. It is one of our psychic mysteries that the displacement of self in some way restores it, and is a prime motivation for invading the bush.

As the sun nears the horizon, however, a curious metamorphosis takes place. Slickrock that had meant smooth walking or a novel slant of light, begins to resemble a kitchen floor. Soft soil suddenly suggests a mattress or a tent site. Boulders that offered obstruction or a lesson in geology are reborn as tables and chairs. Shrubbery is a potential sunscreen, a windbreak, a living room wall. Caves become utility apartments. The lower the sun sinks, the more the wilderness takes on the look of a bourgeois interior, and it becomes clear that part of our mental furniture is still, quite literally, furniture.

Any group of campers will veer in temperament when it is time to select a site, a variation multiplied by the number present. Sand or slickrock? Scenery or shelter? First light from the east or morning shade for sleeping? Would you rather camp above the floodline, where it's safe, or near water, where it's convenient? Do you crave open country or, like me, are you looking for a small space to fill like a hermit crab? Options are advanced in terms of the availability of firewood, the density of bugs, the practicalities. Practicalities, indeed crucial, double as a social mask, and behind the preferred wisdom of each position, consciously or otherwise, lurks each plaintiff's vision of where he or she *really* wants to camp. Just as one's home is a projection of oneself, where one lights for pleasure springs from such compulsions as, say, a wish to sleep in the open or to hide from the moon. And those twists themselves only mediate between the social camper and his innermost drive—the impulse to expand one's ego into the universe, to gather one's fellows into a clan, or to return to the womb. Inside the party about to camp stretches a wilderness from which no psychologist has returned, and an astute gypsy could doubtless learn to read campsites as wickedly as tea leaves or a throw of cards.

Once the spot is picked, personality comes safely into the open. As equipment spills from the pack, the wilderness takes on intimacy, an imagined layout, a sense of habitation variously conceived. A friend of mine who keeps an immaculate two-room house sets up a kitchen with slickrock linoleum, well-vented fireplace, stone shelving and a woodpile graded into kindling, cooking fuel and ornamental flames, while the bedroom is the purest wall-to-wall sand. Another, who operates a county grader, will pull a level and a collapsible shovel from his pack and engineer a personal bedsite so quadrangular and smooth it looks ready for cement. A large flat rock is a predictable battleground between two of my friends, one conscripting it for a kitchen table unless the other grabs it first for his nightly bier. The UNESCO flag makers spend every night in the same nylon pyramid, before which they improvise an elaborate patio on which to sip tea and exclude the neighbors. I ring all of my needs around my sleeping bag to placate laziness, while a still more slovenly friend throws all her junk in a heap and curls up in the middle. Every camper has his own touch at domesticating the wild, and offers an unwitting gaze into himself as he turns his piece of the wilderness into the great indoors.

Some of us can only be pried from the wilds by threat of starvation. Others may experience on, say, the seventh dawn of a ten-day hike, an overwhelming urge to sense the purr of their Siamese against them on their own mattress, the squalling of their children, the hiss of their personal furnace, the proximity of diet cola, the very dust that clings to curtains they can pull shut. As travelers they have ceased to function, and the lag between minds already at home and bodies still lashed to the pack stretches their return into intolerable tedium, filling them with nostalgia for the very routine that may be speeding their life to its end.

If campers are already singletons, it is the last day that

finds them strung farthest apart. One of my own compatriots is notorious for maneuvering the last camp as close as possible to the cars, then rising for a dawn sprint to the Wagoneer with visions of speeding to the nearest hot water and commercial mattress, claiming urgent business obligations. Another has a more immediate goal in the car itself, the can of mandarin oranges she has been brooding on ever since she finished the last mystery. Another will do anything to retard the return, will sit midstream with what remains of the grain alcohol, lift the vial to her lips and go spastic. My own exits vary wildly. Sometimes I can't bear to leave; other times I get to wondering what's in the mail. Once I asked a friend why he was fluttering his fingers so strangely around the last few bends. "Just practicing the guitar," he replied. I had to laugh, because I had myself been running through Dohnányi finger exercises in anticipation of a return to the piano. But whatever one's departing mood, relief to find the car still alive is mixed with a kind of inner shriveling: one's dreary cubist existence is about to resume.

If a night is to be spent en route after the recovery of vehicles I much prefer the truce of a car camp, but am occasionally overpowered by someone in a frenzy for hot water. One heads toward one of those towns that beads a highway dissolving in both directions toward nowhere, visible for miles at night as a kind of blue sunrise, luring the motorist like a species-specific animal trap. Even to the renegade an overlit fortress like Ramada Inn looks suddenly gross, and one settles for one of those dim compounds with weeds in the drive called the Singing Facilities Motel. One cadges ice from the owner, who has to break out his own tray, pours a drink, and draws water for a tub that inevitably turns out to be only a shower. One shampoos, shaves if one is of the persuasion, then heads out for another drink plus steak, salad and dessert on the town. Back to the motel, into the cool dreamt-of sheets. Perchance to sleep. But if one's flesh is tingling and clean, one's belly full, one's vices all caught up, one's civilized itches all scratched, why this sudden dismay? Why does one toss to the growl of thirty-six wheelers, the sirens of an all-night cop show through the wall? Why does the bulb just outside the door pour through the feeble curtains as if one had collapsed under a street light? From whence this malaise? If this is the civilization you couldn't wait to embrace, why are you impatient for the first flush of dawn to sound from the next unit?

Much nonsense has been written about finding oneself in the wilds, as if one had a kind of shadow self lurking like Bigfoot through the trees, but by its very contrast the natural world throws a spotlight on human behavior. One can't expose oneself to the elements unobserved. If a trip's revelations are numb on the way home, they begin to revive in your own living room. As you pull the rubble from your pack, toss your nasties in the hamper and air out your sleeping bag, you reach the treasures you have collected and arrange them on the table. You ready your film to be developed. If you take notes even as grudgingly as I, you run them through a typewriter. You arrange to meet your companions for lunch, and the post-mortems begin.

If you run with roughly the same pack, as I do, there is ample to draw on. Journals are passed around, revised and commented upon. Pictures return, are culled, are inflicted at slide parties. The trip is compared with previous outings, the behavior of people compared from trip to trip. Character assassination runs its course, jokes become legends, intrigues develop over the possible contours of the next excursion. Our own trips have acquired names: Six Came Back, Moroni's Folly, The Trail of the Blue Jewel, Leo's Revenge. Any trek that recedes is a classic in the making.

At this point the trip is more intact than on the last days of its actual life. Dim are the cravings one developed

Bruce Berger

toward the end, forgotten the shameful night in the Singing Facilities Motel. Two weeks of exotic raw material are being slimmed by memory. Discussed, winnowed, refined from separate versions which are themselves gathering shape, the trip enters a collective memory, a common domain, a consensus. The beginning and the end have been trimmed, and the rest returns not as a sprawl of ill-sorted sensation, as it was lived, but sleek and inevitable: a work of art.

The lexicon of wilderness travel has evolved no phrase for the completion of the cycle. But theologians and comparative mythologists, unencumbered by the same humility, years ago isolated, limned and labeled the whole process. They call it death and resurrection.

The
Telling
Distance

The Metaphysical Tent

Bruce
Berger

The metaphysical tent is made of real nylon. It is pitched in clean arroyos, lush meadows, woods on a warm starry night, peaceful streambanks, sandbars and plateaus—anywhere the air is delicious, the stars brilliant and the sounds of darkness busy with a subdued and comforting music. The metaphysical tent is not drawn against weather. It is drawn against snakes, scorpions, tarantulas, kissing bugs, Gila monsters, bears, bats, griffins, pterodactyls, werewolves, voyeurs: all the evil projections and chimeras of the human skull. The metaphysical tent is a sedative, a stiff drink, an all-night station, Mother's nylon arms. It catches the body only by mistake. The body meanwhile suffers sweat, stickiness, musty clothing, jamming of the ear, insomnia, boredom and its own gathering smell. The fearful brain and the captive body cohabit under the metaphysical tent until the red-eye of dawn, when the stakes are pulled, the cords folded in, the nylon rolled and crammed into a stuff bag, the stuff bag loaded into a backpack, and the metaphysical tent steals heavily away.

Sidewinders Anonymous

Some of us do not move very rapidly along the main channel. It is not that our packs are heavy, that we are lazy, that we cannot find our footing, that we cannot decide whether to take the meanders midstream or to shave the corners through the weeds. It is that every few bends there is a breach in the walls, luring us into a darker world which must also be explored.

It is their seduction that a series of side canyons through the same formation are no more alike than we, of standard human flesh, who explore them. I recently spent ten days hiking twenty river miles with fellow canyoneers. By linear standards we were practically at rest, yet we were constantly in motion because of poking into every slot we came to. The first was little more than a recessed seep, ringed by a stand of eight-foot poison ivy red as dried chiles, beneath which a tarantula posed on a rock while I snapped its portrait. The next was one of those dream sagas that began like a great cathedral, snaked for three miles the width of a hotel corridor, gave way to banks of cottonwoods by a running stream, then opened to a gallery of towering formations—which might lead onto the encompassing plateau, or might turn you back after fifteen despairing miles. The third dead-ended after five turns beneath a vaulting double arch, animated by a single bat that circled and circled a dark pool so slow and close one caught its tiny face. The next canyon was so choked with reeds, grasses, watercress, box elders, scrub oak, nettles and stagnant murk one never quite knew what one was stepping on, nor saw what birds cried from the trees. At the next indentation we merely intended to get out of the heat, and found a rattlesnake curled around a limb at eye level, its head nestled peacefully among its soft loops, asleep in the same cool we had sought. Another seeming dead-end continued in a slot so fine we proceeded sideways, spelunking and blind, groping our way to the last shaft. The next was a chasm of rubble. The next . . .

Side canyons, even more than their connecting river, give you a sense of something you can't quite name that leads you on. Smells are musky and herbal, or dry and powdery, touched here with an obscure honeysuckle, there with a whiff like clothes steeped in tobacco smoke. Their very obstacles urge you forward. You will fling off your clothes to get through a cold pool, only to chimney above it with a foothold here, an ass-wedge there, up to the next impediment. Faced with an intractable slot, you will backtrack to the last rockslide, scramble up, then proceed along a high shelf until the canyon rises to meet you. You will shinny up a tree, a rotten ledge, a friend's flesh: anything rather than turn back. Most fiendishly, side canyons have side canyons, which in turn sprout side canyons, and if you have squandered a certain amount of energy in the system already, the urge to completeness takes over. You have to see it all, at whatever cost. You find yourself grabbing precarious knobs, working dubious slots, for the madness of one more bend. The addict will stop at nothing, will risk his living flesh to see which way dumb stone will twist next. The end may be one more wall. Or it may be a glimpse of the mountain lion which has eluded you all your life.

Side canyons almost generate their own laws. Shortly after hearing that owls are considered evil omens, I hiked with a friend in a side canyon of the Escalante River and spotted a large owl asleep in shadow over our heads. We were silent for several minutes hoping he might step forward into sunlight where we could get a better look,

Bruce Berger

and at last my friend tossed a stick against the rock beneath him, to startle him awake. The owl burst out with a great flapping of wings while my camera clicked on blurred stone.

Shortly beyond the canyon forked. It was getting late, time to turn back, and a boulder the size of a garage stood at the confluence, promising a clear view either way. While my friend waited I scrambled up some rocks, leapt onto the boulder and suddenly felt dizzy. I stood still for a moment, waiting for my head to clear, while everything continued in motion. With a shock I realized the entire rock was unsettled by my weight, and was about to topple. I quickly backed off the way I came, regained solid ground, and dizziness gave way to a pounding heart. Out in the mainstream I would never find a connection between a disturbed owl and a treacherous rock. But in a side canyon . . .

The addict knows that to enter a side canyon is to spin the wheel of fortune. His career is a series of tangents, out and back, out and back; like the sidewinder he advances laterally. It does no good to tell him his behavior is about as reasonable as a frayed rope, that his days are a compendium of minutiae, that he cannot see the river for its tributaries. It is useless to appeal to his personal safety. Every unexplored slot is a road not taken, a crossroads ignored, an adventure missed. He is Theseus in the labyrinth, Orpheus in Hades, Uncle Wiggly in search of his fortune, advancing toward he knows not what grail. If his main channel friends tell him he will never get there, he may reply, with his headful of dead-ends, that there is destination in every step.

The Vibram Stomp

Bruce
Berger

The bootprint is a device for turning the human foot into an abstraction. One sees them trailing across the sands—baroque soles with their sunbursts of stars and bars, deck shoe treads like postage cancellations, sneakers like eyes through Sevillian windows. The foot, like other human extremities, is self-expressive and meets the world with a personal touch. In a large party there are seldom two prints alike. The marks of any two persons are distinct and become known, by some unbreakable back country code, as Bigfoot and Littlefoot. By size, configuration and placement, footprints acquire personalities, humanize one's predecessors. One trails like a sleuth, strewing ciphers of one's own.

But for all their suggestiveness, bootprints are not always welcome. Deer paths, coyote prints, javelina pocks, the great peace signs of heron tracks all indicate wild sensibilities. The S-curve of sidewinders returns one to Eden, among the unfallen. But Vibram soles are born in factories. They conspire in closets, foster corns, devour moleskins, demand to be replaced. They are about as alluring as waffle irons. The tread of man, the most dangerous beast of all, paradoxically lessens the shiver of adventure.

Until recently the preferred extension of the human personality was the machine; it still is for a majority. The extension of the foot is the wheel, says Marshall McLuhan, and the woods and dunes are quite full of feet multiplied by wheels. But the romance of the machine is wearing off and the hangover has set in. Most contemporary wilderness travelers wish to banish the machine, to recover their individuality in the age of cybernation. That means getting back to the unaided foot. Unaided, that is, except for the friendly boot.

So today's rebel laces up and sets out to outwalk technology. He seeks a canyon unviolated by previous contemplation, a mesa where original response can flower. He reaches a plateau of windswept contours, embroidered by jackrabbits, stitched by lizards. The shadows of hawks disturb no sand. Suddenly a pair of alien Vibrams stomps to the horizon. Eden is gone; the sons of Euclid are back. Even here, at the last outpost, is the assembly line foot, logo of the human will.

Some objections, of course, are less metaphysical. Hikers trudging through shale and packed mud set off gullies and slides that continue on their own. Vegetation in narrow desert canyons can be mashed wall-to-wall. Public campsites are being chafed into mudflats. School groups and conservation organizations with the noblest intentions can defoliate through sheer numbers, and private parties are close behind. Wind, rain and occasional flooding may erase the rubber stamps, but revegetation is unlikely in areas that cannot be roped off like city parks.

The juniper and piñon country of the Colorado Plateau adds a further problem. Its lumpy red earth, seemingly shaped by the last rain, is actually held in place by microscopic plants called cryptogams. As wind sweeps over the ground it lifts the loose particles, leaving a complex of algae, fungi, lichens, molds and other small growths on tiny pillars, giving the soil a darkish cast. Cryptogams increase the organic carbon content of crust soils, reduce runoff, heighten fertility and keep it all from blowing away. Deer, the only native large animals, file through it on thin trails beaten hard. But campers unaware of its presence scuff it loose at random, and campsites abolish it completely. Of course any damage done by the human

The Telling Distance

foot is negligible compared to meandering cattle which have overgrazed the region for a century. But the cattle know not what they do, while human beings could remove their cows and walk single file, if they so chose.

As we hike from our machines it would be liberating for man and plant if we could simply quit our bodies and explore like wraiths, filling canyons with the sheer enthusiasm of disembodied senses, leaving no local trace even of thought. Realistically, the most we can look forward to is air-cushion shoes. For all our abstraction we are gross mammals, possessed of mass like everything else on this planet. Our hearts are full of adventure but our feet are killing us. This is the price of self-awareness—for the farther we range in search of adventure, the faster we stamp it out.

Bruce
Berger

The Fire Sermon

At the first blush over the rimrock, before the bats have gone to bed, my heart kindles for the first sip of coffee. Into air like chilled crystal I slip from the bag, rush into my clothes and snap the dead tips off the nearest rabbit brush. Then a handful of twigs, a few sticks like fat sausages and a couple of long-burners. Last night's ashes are still warm. I make a pyramid of twigs over the rabbit brush, touch a match and it leaps into flame. Next the sausages, then the grill with a charred pot and a little water. Pungent smoke curls into the sky. By the time the first light touches rock I am taking the first black sip.

Is it the coffee or the dawn? I can feel the day being born inside as lionlight creeps down the wall, touching the sandstone, the slopes of dried grass, the ledges of piñon, sending recesses into deep shadow. The canyon wakens, layer by layer. I let the fire die down, build it back up. By the second cup the sun has splayed the shadow of a nearby juniper onto a pink dune. Miraculously, my campmates are still asleep, and I am afraid even to blow my nose for fear of honking them all awake. By the time sunlight touches my skin I am stirring the third cup: for this is my private coffee ceremony, my way of sending the sun my own responding flame. Or the delusion, at least, of a fire sign.

It was a shock, therefore, to camp for the first time with friends who detest campfires. At first they ignored my pall oozing luxuriously downcanyon, and choked in silence. Then they spoke. Remo, cautious at first, warmed to his topic. "It isn't only the smoke. It's also that fires strip whole areas of their natural dead wood. They leave black scars on the rock. Most people don't dismantle them afterward, so you keep running into these little construction sites everywhere. The peace is shattered by people breaking wood down to size. The smell sticks to your clothes. When the wind changes, your tear ducts ache. A campfire has all the charm of a power plant, shrunk to scale."

Gloria stood silent through this litany, then added, "But what I really can't stand is the way everyone stares at the coals after dinner without saying anything. The fire is the camper's boob tube."

I halfway agreed. I was aware of, even applauded, the ban on fires in parks where entire campgrounds were being denuded and campers were attacking live trees, not to mention the forests bristling with tinder where Smokey the Bear was having his nightly hemorrhage. I never understood why it was necessary to construct a minor Stonehenge merely to cook dinner, and was aware it was no longer fraternal to cede your used pit to the next fellow. When we broke camp I dutifully scattered the rocks, dispersed the unburnt wood to simulate disorder, kicked or buried the ashes, turned stones to their clean sides, and left only a little charred sand for evidence. But I never felt my precious wilderness experience was destroyed by someone's discreet firepit. As for fire's social value, despite Gloria's disclaimer it was the radiant heart of the campsite. It carved a lighted room out of darkness. Around that dance of flame the real communion took place.

I noted with perverse satisfaction the hiss of Remo and Gloria's white gas burner filling the canyon like a far expressway, but I began to hear as well the crash of my own boot on a branch, breaking it into fuel. I began to observe the direction of my smoke, planned my sites downwind, and cringed when a shift swung the smoke toward disapproving nostrils. I saw the emptiness gape from areas

Bruce
Berger

cleared of sticks. I watched insects run from their hideouts, ants crawl from burning logs. I felt the rawness in my eyes while I moved around the fire and smoke followed me like an accusing finger. And I began to resent scrubbing pots whose soot only migrated from aluminum to skin to clothing. I began to consider, abstractly, the alternative.

Some gaseous little device? The burner, with bottles of white gas or cartridges of butane to fuel it, could only displace more enjoyable items from the pack. Unlike fallen timber, they had to be paid for. As machines, they were certain to hate their masters and scheme insurrection mid-omelette. Their odor was noxious, the seethe of jets their answer to crackling wood, their dancing flames a ring of orderly blue teeth. As for my coffee ceremony, I might as well be back at the kitchen range. I pictured ethical campers sitting in a ring around their pooled burners, baring their small souls . . .

In the larger context, burners were made of metal that had to be prospected, mined, smelted, assembled and shipped. The gas had to be explored, drilled, refined and transported. The finished amalgamation was advertised and sold. The burner, one tiny wart on the corporate octopus, saved some exquisite backpackers' corner while sacking the world at large. In currently chic vocabulary, the traditional campfire, using a local renewable resource, was soft technology, while burners embodied the massive, discredited hard stuff.

More personally, fire, for those who grew up in its glow, retains its sacramental magic. It is a last link with our pioneer tradition. It was by Prometheus' theft of divine fire that mankind rivaled the gods. Heraclitus, predating the classical Greek philosophers, proclaimed all creation a form of fire, and the dancing patterns of contemporary physics find him metaphorically in concert. From ortho-doxy to alchemy, fire is the agent of transformation, the progress of the soul, and a rack of votive candles in a dark alcove gladdens even my own agnostic heart. If today's backpacker is seeking in the wilderness some lost whole-ness, he seems incomplete reduced to earth, water, air and the ether of thought.

But Remo and Gloria's dissent gnawed like slow poi-son. Fire, I realized, was a viable soft technology when there were great expanses of open lands, a sparse popula-tion of Native Americans and a beginning influx of pio-neers. Nature's tolerance was not exceeded. But with the eradication of wilderness and the exponential increase in camping, the ratio is reversed. Dead wood is not renew-able at the rate it is being used, nor is wilderness left looking wild. The untamed should be messy, and we pyromaniacs are in danger of turning it into a pruned garden.

Those of us en route to the wilds are thus caught between ethics. The lore of the pioneer is still canonized by such institutions as the Boy Scouts and the Girl Scouts—not to mention the Campfire Girls—and for males the ability to produce flame in all circumstances is almost a test of machismo. The image of brave souls gentling the night with fire still haunts a spectrum from hunters to backpackers to professors of American art. But the maker of campfires is beginning to feel like the indoor smoker. Subject to individual mandates, local conditions and changing personnel, open flames are being banned from our national parks, or restricted to tight compounds. Regulations are sufficiently fierce that one feels like a junkie who must be monitored if he cannot be redeemed. For the moment one can repair to national forest, BLM or private land which has not been posted, but the message is clear. Fire, as an ingredient of wilderness camping, is an endangered species.

At Christmas Remo and Gloria, my clean-burning friends, sent me an incriminating photo showing my campfire filling a canyon with smog. When my retaliatory verses signed Smokey the Unbearable sounded a little lame, I took the plunge and invested, against every instinct, in a nasty little burner. I tested it at home, found it made heat with minimal stink and packed it—mainly out of curiosity—into the desert.

I was first struck by an unexpected burst of freedom. Absolved of the search for firewood, the location and construction of the pit, cuisine by committee and the final unblacking of pots, time opened up for serious lounging. I was free to camp on the margins, socialize at will and retreat to my lair. The hiss of jets was brief, and gave way to the sifting of wind and the night cries. My eyes, no longer glued to the tube, adjusted to silhouettes and stars. The burner did take room in my pack otherwise occupied by, say, a little more rum, or glorious empty space, and my back was not enchanted with the three fuel cartridges. Nor can I claim that social life was enhanced with most of the party off cooking by themselves. But heat was instantaneous and without guilt: I was Prometheus unbound.

My sacred dawns, of course, were low on sacrament. First light touched rimrock without the pungency of juniper smoke, the ceremony of an answering flame. Virtue triumphed over romance. But there is another sacrament in sparing wood that has lived a thousand years and has become, in death, the protector of scorpions, termites, centipedes and their brethren. If those creatures can adapt to the desert, perhaps I can too.

Heat

—unlike cold—is one of those pleasures most keenly relished on the threshold of pain. It is oddly comforting to feel noon pouring down, to bake from beneath over bedrock, to find your marrow vaguely radiating. The best midsummer lunch is to gorge on enchiladas blazing with chiles, return to the car you have left in the sun with the windows rolled up, lock yourself in to steep in your own tears and sweat, then step out to find the heat wave has turned delicious. It is invigorating to walk over simmering gravel, feeling your soles come alive as they toughen, and baths are most relaxing when they resemble the first stages of missionary stew. Perhaps it is a desire to return to the womb, where we began for nine months at 98.6, that makes the warmth of alcohol so seductive, and one can comprehend—if not envy—the uncomforted who go through life sucking the eighty proof tit.

Bruce Berger

To test my heat tolerance I once went into the desert when daytime temperatures were easing off around 107 degrees, to see what might transpire. I expected an escort of insects, lizards, snakes, scorpions and chuckawallas, all the cold-blooded predators warmed like me for action, but the cactus stood in stunned silence. The afternoon lay like a ruin through which I seemed the only moving thing. My eyes ran with salt, my thirst became pathological, and I fled homeward to chug two beers nonstop before I could explain myself. But did I dream of cool mountains, as I did in childhood? No. It is as an adult, exiled to cool mountains, that I dream of the desert.

Desert Moon Hotel

P erhaps it was the sign with the moon grinning and
winking just over the front door that gave the two-
story frame house set back in the foliage its look of minor
adventure. Every time I passed through Thompson, Utah,
I thought about stopping for the night—and sped on. But
with the new interstate re-routing coast-to-coast traffic a
mile south of town, no doubt dooming the hotel, adventure could not be put off, and I found myself pushing open
a door labeled Office and walking into a skinny, creaking
hall where a man with his back to me stood talking to the
proprietress at a registration window. He turned, pushed
past me toward the front door and said, "Your turn," as if
freeing a urinal, leaving me to face a plain-looking middle-
aged woman with straight cropped hair.

"I'd like a room for tonight."

"There's only one left."

"I'll take it."

She pushed a registration blank toward me. "Are you
losing much business with the traffic out on the fourlane
now?" I asked.

"Not now. We're full of construction workers."

"How about when the highway's finished?"

"We're out on the highway now."

"You've got a sign out there?"

"No, a cafe and a trailer court. That's $5.35."

I paid, got change. "If you want to eat, the best place
here is the Kamp Kourt Cafe."

"Your place?"

"Yes," she replied without humor. "Here's the key to number five. Up the stairs, in front."

I decided to pry one more fact. "When was this place built?"

"Nineteen thirty-four. But the sheets are clean."

Keyhole number five took the key through a series of baffles, any one of which might have meant business, clinking nakedly in the hall's silence. Then the door gave way to a cubicle full of dust and pine smells bursting with memories. A small double bed, a black and white dresser missing a drawer, a silver radiator, a monumental floor-to-ceiling armoire of knotty pine: those basic appointments were complemented by a cracked mirror framed in oak, curtains of some heavy material patterned with roses and marble feathers, and a bas-relief plaster pistol of a piece with its frame. Offering diversion were a paperback of *Helter Skelter,* a copy of *True* and another magazine called *Man's World,* which turned out to be full of split beavers.

Bruce
Berger

But the real entertainment was a window situated so that you could sit in bed and watch the last sun on Book Cliffs, that banded shale that stretches like a wall of crumpled bats across northern Colorado and Utah. I poured a little scotch to deepen the shadows, and primarily to ease my stomach from having eaten something called a Blazing Saddle in Glenwood Springs several hours back. I would not be sampling the Kamp Kourt Cafe.

Suddenly there came a great roar. A double engine, dirty yellow, screamed into view, pulling dozens of heaping black Union Pacific coal cars. It slowed, agonized to a stop, trembling like an exhausted python in either direction. After a few minutes a bold E7 announced another train, also from the east, hauling racks of shiny new Datsuns, then a file of empty boxcars that may have represented every line in America. After it passed, the first train gave a tentative lurch, groaning like a creature in pain as each car snapped taut with a separate jolt. As it lumbered out I realized that no image of galactic travel, exploding universes or space-time continua can conjure sheer distance like a departing train.

The sun went down and a cottonwood rustled like taffeta across the tracks. Softly a piano, with that rich, slurred tone distilled in Chicago uprights around the turn of the century, began Scott Joplin's "The Entertainer," bungled a few bars of boogie, attempted Beethoven's "Für Elise" and settled for Joplin. When the musician gave up I reached for a volume from my incomplete Complete Conrad, and turned for reasons of atmosphere to a tale called "The Inn of the Two Witches."

Suddenly the construction crew burst through the front door. Every floorboard, door and drawer resounded like the parchment of a drum, transmitting sound rather than deadening it, booming and reverberating in all directions. Boots on stairs shook the entire frame. Conversations were public statements, dealt in that Western twang in which language seems continually to be stumbling over its own feet. There were, mercifully, no radios, no TVs. Someone started whistling "The Entertainer," shortening all the intervals, shifting keys at random. The whistler persisted through two rounds of the cuckoo clock, then lumbered on heavy feet downstairs, trailed by all the other feet. The wailing of the wind was the only sound left. I was drifting off when the floor-shattering feet stumbled back around midnight, without conversation. The last sound I registered was another train, boring deeply into the night.

When I woke the marble-feathered curtains were brightly lit, the Blazing Saddle was digested and the construction crew had gone. The Book Cliffs were dancing with purples and mauves, and I felt reborn. Yet next time I would probably push on to the drab, overlit motels where one can withdraw from contact and read Conrad in peace. That is what is so terrible about our fourlane culture: even as it shrugs our old bivouacs aside, it drains us of the will to discover.

The Silent Elite

The evilest cliché currently suffered by wilderness defenders is that of elitism. The word is conveniently vague, but means variously that foot-travelers are rich, offensively young and healthy, selfish, snobbish, and members of an aspiring cabal.

These charges have been answered at length, but to recapitulate: hiking and backpacking are necessarily cheap since after the initial outlay for equipment, gas to reach the wilds, and food to survive, there *is* no place to spend money. The youth argument is dispelled by the number of aging Sierra Clubbers on the trail—and they have probably *stayed* on the trail because of all the exercise it gave them. Selfishness? Machine fanciers now have access to ninety-seven percent of American lands south of Alaska; if the other side is selfish for declining to compromise the remaining three percent, the word selfish needs redefinition. In matters of snobbery, the trailbikers look down on the birdwatchers and the birdwatchers look down on the joggers and there is nothing gained by measuring decibels. As for power, anyone who has compared Earth First! with Exxon knows where might lies.

But having dismissed elitism, I would like to salvage one aspect and boast of it: whenever I stumble onto some secret natural treasure, I try to keep quiet. I say try, because the first instinct is to show it off like a prize arrow, to drag a friend or group of friends there to admire it, to experience it multiplied through others' delight. But the upshot is obvious: they would tell their friends, who would tell

Bruce Berger

their friends, and the squads would descend. Secret sharers are rare, and seldom keep their mouths shut once you have opened your own.

I once spent a week with a party of seven in a canyon free of a single footprint, a scrap of litter, all trace of human passage except for a migration tag that had fallen off a mountain lion, a few ancient petroglyphs, and the jet trails from which no contemporary sky is immune. With sandstone formations soaring above us we threaded pine forests, fields of wildflowers, a stone labyrinth, pools lively with trout, and even came upon a small geyser, all fresh as if humanity were newly minted. The going was rough and we may never return, yet we swore to each other—an oath I believe we have kept—never to refer to it publicly except as Moroni's Folly, and never to hint at its location. We *are* cliquish, but the fact is that we watched our fourteen boots blaze an incipient trail, stamp out lichen that takes decades to recover, and sheer away entire banks of emerald moss where there was no other way through. A friend who has been generous with her own secrets is rightfully resentful that I will not divulge Moroni's Folly, but she is a trip leader for a national conservation organization and I shiver at the prospect of all those well-meaning feet. If we were the elite, the elite was all Moroni's Folly could take.

It is well known that our favored American wildlands are being stomped into mudflats: in the popular phrase, loved to death. It is better to die for love than for a stripmine or a reservoir, but damage is damage. For those who treasure some personal hideout, secrecy is a way of defending it for personal enjoyment—but also for its own survival. The ultimate protection might be for wilderness lovers to stay home, but who is willing? Love is not consummated at a distance, and the urge to explore, reports Arthur Koestler, is becoming recognized as a drive equal to hunger and sex. Drives are quite incurable and the overpopulation of our exploratory selves, of course, is the ultimate culprit. But just as our sex drive must be geared

The
Telling
Distance

for the least production, so must our explorations minimize the damage. And potent in our arsenal of defense is a fine silence.

The joy of such elitism is that it yields a surprise dividend. The entire surface of our globe is currently being mapped by Telstar. U. S. Geological Survey maps are completing their account of our last geological deformity, and in one extensive Western canyon the Bureau of Land Management is preparing a guide to the Anasazi ruins, to be numbered in the hundreds. The hiker who used to catch his breath when a kiva took shape from a cliff will now stumble downcanyon with his nose in a guidebook, wondering how he missed Ruin No. 163. Our killjoy tax dollars at work.

Bruce Berger

A computer may get its greatest thrill from completing a data bank, but most of poor flawed human joy has its roots in surprise. Beauty does not gain from programming. Let those who savor the wilds go out and find their own secrets, relish them and keep them. Such is the elitism of democracy: that we all have access to the elusive, the equal opportunity to be obscure. Let us treasure our private corners, and fend them from the armies of earth-lovers like ourselves. By playing a close hand we'll let our fellows make their own discoveries, and keep a little mystery—and mystery's joy—in the world. I will try to find out all you know, but don't be fooled. I promise not to tell you some of my secrets if you promise not to tell me some of yours.

Dope in the Desert

Our thighs were of marble, our kneecaps were missing, our calves were like rain-shrunk clothesline: we had spent two days working our way down the wrong canyon. Over us loomed tier upon tier of crumbling sandstone, barberry thickets, slots, plunges and configurations we couldn't square with the hotly debated map, and which belonged (oops!) not to the mysterious gorge none of us had been to, but to a side canyon of the system we explored last year. Still it was pleasant to be lounging on a terrace of slickrock, watching a pool of cattails and vermilion dragonflies, licking our physical and spiritual wounds. At eleven Gloria broke out the grain alcohol, and at one Carmen produced a little plastic bag full of an odd raspberry powder.

Dope in the desert? Some now-forgotten Yippie once remarked that not to drop acid was to betray one's generation, and during the sixties I took a couple of required mescaline flights, lest I be accused of counter-revolution. The sharpened taste and suspension of time were curious if less reassuring than scotch on the rocks. But what, I sometimes wondered, if I hadn't been at home but out in the canyons, in the desert, in the country I love? Might that be the mystic combination? I licked my little finger and dipped it into Carmen's Baggie.

We continued to admire the dragonflies and crack puns while nothing in particular happened. At three I tried another hit. The raspberry was sickeningly sweet. At five it became clear my system was depressingly straight.

But I promised Robin and Carmen to try again, and next morning, after coffee, I dutifully wandered over to their shelf, took three healthy licks off my finger and set off for the day. I dawdled in alcoves, turned upstream at the main canyon, and found Robin and Carmen had hiked ahead of me to a pool where they intended to spend the day. "I think you've been had by your pusher," I remarked.

"I think not," replied Carmen. "Give it one more lick."

Several turns beyond their pool I heard a flicker quietly tapping a cottonwood, and sat down to watch. Even in such stillness it seemed remarkable to hear so precisely a creature so far and small, to see the black vee on its neck as if through binoculars. I felt a sweet tightness in my throat, a sense of drawstrings pulling extremities taut. My heart was excited yet calm, like a racer in training. I looked around.

Bruce Berger

The canyon was newly vast, filled with the minutest particulars, yet small enough to encompass in a single eyespan. If I fixed on a particular rock, a juniper, stain or shadow, its character was as isolated as a slide under a microscope. But I was simultaneously aware of the macrocosm, the way the canyon represented a single wedge through stacked layers of rubble, rockface and vegetation, the way the two sides were like warped mirrors, and especially the way a major fault would slice down one side, provoke a riffle in the streambed and continue into a side canyon. My eye accepted whichever stress I chose, geology as structure or as heap of gargoyles. This was not hallucination but hyper-reality—with one odd change. This particular system with its layers of shale, its crumbling ashiness, its floor of dark limestone, had always suggested a prospect of decaying brownstones, some industrial brick city falling into its coal-smeared basement. Yet here were the selfsame layers all cheerfully pink and steam and white, jumbled and tossed like ill-stacked poker chips.

The flicker had long since gone, I had stock of my new

senses, and ambled on. Having survived mescaline at home I felt comfortable with the sensations in the wild, and found my ability to speak, gauge distance and negotiate rock unimpaired. And what of my hands? I took out my notebook, completed a sentence that had been interrupted the day before, and found my handwriting no worse than usual. But it was hard to discipline myself to controlled experiments when my eyes kept veering away. If I looked up, a diagonal fault slashed its way from the rim to my feet. If I looked down, a clump of windblown grass blades drew concentric rings around themselves in the sand: a green target. At one point I was stopped by an effect of New York action painting, of artfully splashed enamel, on the rock. Ideas, phrases, flashes of people meanwhile shot through my brain too fast to inspect and are (no doubt mercifully) lost.

I wandered upstream for hours, barely making tracks, and since I don't wear a watch, I had no measure of time beyond the sun's position. When the sky clouded I became concerned that with little sense of light's passing I might get caught by the October nightfall. Could I actually have traveled a few miles? The novelty was wearing off, and I was anxious now for the cycle to run its course and leave me my knowledge of time and distance.

I reached a formation where the water emerged from the rock. Above here the canyon was dry; it was an obvious turnaround. The moisture sprang from a small cavelike opening, and on a whim I crawled into a space barely the width of myself, rich, dank, almost icy. I wriggled ten feet to the end and peered into darkness, imagining water oozing for miles in a soft sheet over the harder level beneath, making a buried migration that led precisely here. Water fanning through darkness—I could envision it. No, not quite. In an effort to use the drug I was forcing the experience, crawling into this hole for some literal insight. But real insight occurs like water to a more casual observer, springing unbidden.

As I loitered homeward I thought about those who use drugs creatively. Was I potentially one of them? The expanded field of vision might be fine for someone who wanted to think structurally, the geologist or the physicist, and the emergent patterns might particularly inspire the artist. While it is hard to picture the Audubon Society on LSD, the intensification of sight and sound might be useful for birding, or the study of animal behavior. But experience particularizes, whereas language abstracts. And all day as I wandered this compendium of stacked particulars and veined minutiae, I did not make a single new connection. I thought about essays in progress that might pertain—the one about footprints, the one about tamarisk—but nothing curious occurred, and the only material to work with, in fact, might be an account of the experience itself. An adept might learn to sort it all out, to isolate what he wanted, but my own thoughts were often more inspiring on the second beer. It was an experience I might repeat in the right circumstance, but I would never seek it out. And considering the risks to the taker, including the legalities, the temptation is slight.

Bruce Berger

With my eye on the clouds and awareness that time had to be passing, dusk still took me by surprise and I returned to camp at nightfall. Those unaware I had dipped into the raspberry noticed no oddness of behavior. Had I had an interesting day? Oh yes, I had watched a flicker, and seen where water came out of a rock . . .

Next morning, feeling no ill effects, I indulged in a few post-mortems. The sentence I had completed in my notebook was so uniformly ill-written that I couldn't find the break. And the canyon walls did show some red, but not very much. "The drug activates the red cones of our eyes," explained Carmen, "and gives them undue prominence." But the color of any object is composed of the light it rejects, reconstructed in the observer. Is the canyon sooty or red? That depends less on the canyon than ourselves.

"So was it worth it?" asked Robin.

"Sure," I said, "though hardly what I expected when we came down the wrong canyon."

"That's because there *are* no wrong canyons," he commented.

The Telling Distance

Wilderness Temperament

Bruce
Berger

It is one of our romantic American notions that one can "find oneself" in the wilderness, a self obscured by the entanglements of town. After several decades of journeying in the wild, I find the self is just as elusive as ever, and suspect that as a kind of psychic bedrock it may not even exist. On the way to this non-discovery, however, I may have run across an aspect of personality that can be pinned down, that varies from person to person, and that expresses one's attitude toward the outdoors. Less grand than one's "self," it might be called one's wilderness temperament.

These thoughts were churned up by a trip I recently made in a party of thirteen down a Southwestern river. Only once before had I been on an actual river trip, a two-week float through Glen Canyon before its annihilation by Lake Powell. That experience of Glen Canyon was overwhelming, and a minor drawback comes back only now. Idyllic as it was to float the Colorado River between massive tapestried walls, I felt vaguely imprisoned by our rubber raft. More vivid were the times we worked our way up side canyons, or clambered slickrock to the rim. In retrospect, I realize I was far happier on rock than on water.

On the recent river trip, more than twenty years later, I was given command of a Sportyak, a tiny one-man plastic rowboat, part of an armada that included two more Sportyaks, three kayaks, two rubber pontoons, and a canoe. I was told and then shown how it worked.

Childhood rowing instincts came back, and I even enjoyed bobbing over small stationary waves the river folk referred to as "haystacks." On the second morning I was advised to stay close behind a more experienced yakker, for the river would get eventful. When the yakker yelled "That's it!" over the noise of the water, I figured I was doing it right.

A moment later I realized that what the yakker had yacked was "Rapids!" The little boat I meant to keep facing forward swung magnetically toward a rock mid-river, swerved around it, spun into a hole beneath it, emerged backward, and was swamped by the wave below the hole. A series of giant haystacks followed, each trying to pour more water into my full load. The boat was too heavy to spin forward again, and rather than take the waves sideways and overturn, I kept the boat facing backward. Below the rapids the party pulled out to catch its breath. I was congratulated for having come through rightside up, and was assured that by keeping the boat backward I had exercised control. What I felt, along with adrenaline and a sense of fatalism, was that I'd been wholly at the river's mercy, and that any congratulations were due the makers of the unsinkable Sportyak. And past the post-mortem loomed a broader issue: what had all this frantic nautical activity to do with the country I'd come to see?

As the trip splashed on, distinctions between water folk emerged. A Sportyakker who did overturn pronounced it the best moment of the trip. Another so loved the act of rowing that he kept a rowing machine in his living room. One pontoon rider felt the river wasn't challenging enough to bother with in a kayak, so why not keep dry and drink beer? Another had tried all forms of craft, and found fulfillment in a canoe. I most enjoyed my hike up a sandstone fin, and was happiest afloat when I could adjust the view with one oar. Our party expressed thirteen attitudes toward travel by water.

I began comparing river travel with the two other

unmechanized ways I had entered the wilderness: by foot and by mule. Mules, like boats, make constant demands on your attention. The effort of kicking, yelling, and making fearful noises with a switch seemed far more exhausting than walking, and I remember the look of a friend who jabbed with his heels, swore, and kept yelling back, "Is he moving? Is he moving?" For all our exertion, the animals moved more slowly than we could have on our own, and after the first trip I let the beast haul my gear and walked unencumbered.

As for backpacking, we all know the way it intensifies earthly gravity. Backpacking is awkward, ugly, monotonous, and lacks thrilling bodily sensations. On the other hand, I have never had a breeze spin my backpack the wrong way as I trained my binoculars on a snowy egret. I have never raised my camera, only to have the backpack lurch forward and cause the shutter to click on pure sky as I became tangled in reins, camera strap, hat strap, loose glasses, riding crop, and rage. Disengage from a backpack and it will not bolt or float away. It asks only that you haul it from here to there, and leaves you free to pick up rocks, stalk birds, compose pictures or paragraphs, finger lichen, or let your thoughts seep into the ground. Devoid of glamor, it is pure access.

If wilderness is a place where one can blur, for a time, the confines of the ego, the modes of wilderness travel would seem to offer a general choice between dissolving into the fabric of nature or into sensations of the body. River running, mountain climbing and cross-country skiing, at one extreme, nerve the traveler toward challenge, endurance, and physical excitement, and wilderness offers full scope for pushing flesh to the limit. The attitudes on our recent trip, for all their variety, tended to regard the sinews of water as the chief attraction, and the surrounding strata as pleasant background. Pack animals occupy a cumbersome middle ground, while backpacking represents the opposite extreme: transportation one withstands

Bruce Berger

simply to get there. The mode one prefers—one's wilderness temperament—is no more logical than a preference for forest cake or hot peppers, but river runners savor the kinks of tumbling water and alternate craft, while backpackers plan one plod after another. Without regretting a trip I have taken, I know that I am, at heart, a servile backpacker.

As self-knowledge, the determination of one's wilderness temperament may fall short of enlightenment. But if one does not truly find oneself, at least one will not find oneself on the wrong trip.

The
Telling
Distance

Wilderness Camp

"I've got it," says the backpacker in a ventriloquial baritone, gesturing over a sweep of pines, crags, and plummeting streams. "We'll put the Ramada Inn over here, the Fotomat on that unfinished spire, run the business route through that draw . . ." The ironist stands on Vibram soles. He shoulders a pack of aluminum tubing and rip-stop nylon, dense with goose-down bedding and clothing, pot nest, butane burner, dehydrated food, binoculars and camera. He has gotten beyond city streets by means of the car he left at the trailhead. As if ready for a spacewalk, he has cut the umbilical from Mother Technology only after she has packed his lunch—and he knows it. Irony, that flower of civilization, now runs through the wilderness like ragweed.

Bruce Berger

The impersonation of developers, whose mania is really beyond satire, is only a tedious running joke. Backpackers fortunately have developed a far defter strain in which bits of civilization are torn from their sockets and played against a primitive setting. The game is suppressed during the day, when hikers are immersed in the ruggedness they came for. But by sundown, exhausted by all that purity, the hiker needs to let go. He is still civilized at heart, and the rigors of communing with nature give way to a brand of self-parody that gives new meaning to the phrase *camping out.*

The obvious target is food, a jest quite understood by outfitters who offer a rainbow of disks and crystals that rehydrate into meat stroganoffs, seafood creoles, poultry

Tetrazzinis, ingots of compressed bacon and fruit cobblers for people who subsist, like Americans, on hamburgers and fish stix back home. But cuisine in tinfoil is only the beginning. Once the fire is built or the burner primed, out come the film cans of sherry or Cointreau, the packets of marjoram or thyme, to give rehydration that personal touch. Nouveller still is to add mushrooms, wild onions, or watercress that have been culled when your friends weren't looking, or foliage stalked in memory of Euell Gibbons. By the time sunset brands the rimrock, travelers who have spent the day eroding their feet are settling into a round or two of grain alcohol daiquiris, garnished with wild mint someone spotted by a spring. As daylight dies the aluminum pot disgorges crab gumbo or chicken Marsala, followed by cherries jubilee. With luck the elegance spills over to breakfast, when the dread powdered eggs are laced with leftovers for the kinds of omelette never encountered twice. The basic ingredients may still be chemicals from a factory, but the trekkers are saying to themselves, and possibly each other: here we are in the howling wilderness, having better fare than the folks in town.

The portage from camp to camp opens the field of exterior decoration—a nightly adaptation to deep forests, to water-sculpted canyons, with possibilities unknown in the cube of one's home. Tents are angled so as to command the View, or to convert slickrock into a front porch. Bedrolls in the open are set between clumps of paintbrush and sego lilies, so that the sluggard sipping rum in bed may savor the colors and scents (while looking as if he were disporting in a casket). Pack rats and garage salers love a pocked wall in which to set their cup, flask, flashlight and nail clippers like saints in their niches. Litter, despised by day, is pressed into service: a battered plank elevated into a sideboard, an old tire turned windscreen for a butane burner. A friend who scorns dishwashing compromises with elegance by setting his paper plates inside a frisbee. Fire builders may bypass the classic ring of stones for something longer, more linear, as if in the spell of Frank Lloyd Wright. I have seen a cliffside prickly pear whose extended pad was turned by a candle into a wall sconce—and many a terraced pool used for a split-level cocktail party. Even rain-soaked campers, airing equipment, show proportion in trimming the junipers with burgundy sleeping bags, orange ponchos, cerulean parkas and day-glo socks, until the campsite flashes like a suburban Christmas. By wilderness ethics any barbarism is permitted as long as all constructions are dismantled, vegetation is damaged as little as possible, and the encampment vanishes afterward like a mirage.

The most telling encounters between the manufactured and the wild may occur when humor is the last thing in mind. On one occasion we were to join friends down a little-visited canyon that included a kind of sandstone bowels, squeezing the runoff to pools of unknown depth and requiring us to swim with our packs ahead of us on flotation devices. We made the rounds of the sports stores and found the official backpackers' air mattresses all overweight and overpriced. In desperation we invaded a two-acre dime store and combed the aisles until our eyes lit on a thin box depicting a matron with teased-up red hair, fondling a rosy-cheeked cherub in a round, candy-striped plastic kiddie pool. Its inflatable tubes were designed to hold water rather than to keep it out, but mightn't it serve as a small boat? It weighed almost nothing. We paid almost nothing.

A week later we entered a radiant canyon without a scrap of litter, a previous footprint, any sign of humanity save each other. We dropped over pitches we could never climb back up, and our only way out lay ahead. We reached the first major pool, locked between sheer walls and curving like a charred intestine around the bend. Our friends blew up their olive-drab regulation mattresses. In secret panic I reached into my pack and pulled out our

Bruce
Berger

piece of limp plastic, formless except for two white valves. I huffed, and a great tube lurched into shape. I stoppered it and blew up the other tube. The picture on the box, cluttered with mother and child, hardly did justice to this dazzling rose window of raspberry and peppermint spirals gleaming under a cobalt Utah sky. The entire party was convulsed.

But our lives were at stake. We solemnly read the guarantee from the Ideal Toy Manufacturing Company, Taiwan, insuring the durability of our kiddie pool for two years of "normal use." Could we sue if it sank our packs? We lowered the first pack into the hull, then placed the other gently on top. The cargo rode high and clean between the tubes, just as we'd pictured in the dime store. It blundered forward as we splashed through the icy water. Over dry stretches I was forced to carry the pool on my head so that the tubes fell below my shoulders, rendering me blind as an umbrella table. Of its own accord the pool slipped backward, caught the top of my pack, and surrounded me with a pink nimbus. Friends were so entertained they could barely steady their cameras. When we look back years later on that week full of ponderosas, scarlet walls, wild orchids, wilder descents and black water, the entire canyon is evoked for us by that piece of dime store plastic that became known as the rubber duck.

The Telling Distance

Sliest of all are effects of clothing and possessions, casually on display. There is the little hand mirror whose obverse features a portrait of our Bullmoose President and the inscription, "Teddy Is Good Enough For Me." There are the little boxes of matches from the best restaurant one frequents. There are the inevitable hats with tail feathers, parkas with patches, visors with decals, embroidered camera straps, the more interesting sneakers whose grape shoelaces have been calculated for their vibration against blue nylon. A friend carries his bourbon in a detergent bottle labeled Joy, cured with vinegar and soda "to get out the lemon taste." Another found a disk of metal like a dog tag, bearing a number and the message, "when found, please return with skull." No skull was to be found and an experiment involving bighorn sheep or mountain lions apparently misfired, but she extended its possibilities by affixing the tag to her necklace.

The quest for baroque paraphernalia has not been lost on backpack emporiums, which offer, at satiric prices, such exotica as mica lanterns, collapsible wine glasses, pre-moistened towels, waterproof match holders and spice racks the size of contact lens kits. Sometimes I have found a trinket so irresistible I have bought it and hauled it into the wilds, only to find it too clever or too flimsy to work. Others must concur, for cute gadgetry remains on the market for about a year, and only freeze-dried cuisine—a glorified necessity—seems a constant seller. If today's camper is too sophisticated to take his outings without humor, he is usually too sophisticated to buy his humor from an entrepreneur.

Bruce
Berger

Susan Sontag, in her essay "Notes on 'Camp' " from *Against Interpretation,* describes camp as "Dandyism in the age of mass culture." Camp, she observes, is an attitude that turns life into theater. "Camp sensibility is alive to a double sense in which things can be taken," and "many of the objects prized by Camp are old-fashioned, out-of-date, *démodé.*" Sontag is talking, of course, about the contemporary urban dweller—but the majority of today's backpackers *are* urbanites let loose in a primitive setting. And Wilderness Camp, to extend the terminology, is the art of seeing nature double—as itself and as a play on the civilization left behind.

Humor, it is said, is often wish in disguise. The sensibility that looks to nature for relief from our cluttered and violent times, may also look to a past that was serene, ceremonious, and livable. Wilderness Camp, even for urban renegades, may be a passing mood, but the savor of liqueur and the chill of night air, felt simultaneously, offer a delicious kind of relief. It is triumphant to feel, however briefly, that civilization has not merely been escaped, merely satirized, but outdone. And behind Wilderness Camp, unexpressed, may lurk a significant vision: the dream of cultured flowers with their roots in real earth. Isn't that the mix our transcendentalists endlessly prescribe? Today's camper may not take his nature straight, but irony too has its message. There is more in the woods than humor if, for an instant of exquisite well-being, the extremities of culture and wilderness touch in a true Garden: not without applejack, not without snakes.

*The
Telling
Distance*

Daphne of Dark Canyon

Young Daphne, recently graduated from Prescott College, was out for her first camping solo when Apollo, staring into the canyon, caught her skinny-dipping in a pothole and became inflamed with desire. As Daphne stretched her bedroll along a sandbar that dusk, Apollo, returned from his labors, disguised himself as the river, pulling strength into his tributaries from every passing cloud. Daphne, waking to the roar of the god upon her, trembled and quaked in her desperation to crawl from the bag, until panic turned her blood to wood, her fingers to quivering leaves. And so, my camp friends, when you see a young cottonwood wound in sticks and mud as if caught in a flash flood, you will know that it is only poor Daphne struggling from her bedroll, her fear escaping into the wind.

Bruce Berger

Wilderness and the Buried Self

Travelers back from the wilderness may remark that their trip "passed like a dream" and—as if it were a good night's sleep—that they "hope it lasts." Such phrases may be tossed off without thought of the literal content, but off-hand remarks often carry freights of meaning not consciously intended by their speakers, and folk expressions wouldn't have gained currency without a certain resonance. Wilderness addicts are often accused of emotionalism and irrationality. It may be that instead of denying it they should look to their very unreason as a source of strength—and that they ought to ask themselves, in particular, why their experience of the wilds so often invokes the language of sleep.

One's state in the wilderness is anything but drowsy. The very fundamentals—cooking, finding water, getting through the night, keeping warm or cool, staying safe— cannot be taken for granted. Traveling with a life-support system on one's back and uncertain terrain underfoot, the hiker must watch where to step, keep the load adjusted, and arrive at a reasonable campsite by nightfall. Weather, so easily corrected by a thermostat back home, constantly intrudes with heat, rain, cold, wind, even snow, thunderstorms and flash floods. In tight situations the very basics can compete for attention, requiring a multiplicity of focus otherwise demanded only in fast traffic. Few moments in the wilderness are allowed to pass unnoticed, and it is no wonder that a week in the woods, enjoyed or endured, seems equivalent to three or four weeks at home.

But urbanites do not seek out wilderness to stretch time or complicate the basics; they go to immerse themselves in another context. The more our lands are surfeited by our presence, the more the forces that spawned us retreat from sight. As landscape without our image recedes, the wilds only deepen in their strangeness. Many, of course, have so adapted to mechanized surroundings that they view the elimination of nature with perfect indifference, as if it didn't involve them, or as if concern for the wilds were a comic aberration. But even those whose alienation from nature produces a hunger for it, deepening its allure, find that evolving civilization has given new meanings to nature itself, increasing its psychic remoteness.

The more we clear forests, for instance, the more the remaining ones surround us with sounds we no longer recognize, coming from mysterious densities. Mountain vistas, traditional sources of inspiration, take on extra-terrestrial connotations in this dawn of space exploration. The serpentine webs of canyons, with their water-smoothed knobs, recesses and clefts, may suggest some Freudian underworld. Shifts of climate and terrain add unaccustomed turnings of the irrational. The very unfolding of a trip—across streams, through valleys, over passes—assumes aspects of a fable. Backpackers file through non-civilized country more exiled than their forebears, open to increasing dislocation. Their mental state is alert and receptive, with the ego largely in abeyance. The self may assert itself in relation to other campers, but gives way in the face of the non-human. That waking trance, in which one is lifted out of oneself and included in something larger, was extolled in the last century as Transcendence. Its very existence—so inconvenient to those with more lucrative plans for the wilds—has been denied by exploiters and developers. But for many the sensation remains a crucial part of their lives, and is known in current jargon as the Wilderness Experience.

Sleep itself, after the buffetings of fresh air, exercise,

Bruce Berger

unaccustomed sights, and relief from social pressures, resembles a blackout. Only a novice is tortured by roots and rocks that erupt under bedrolls, or by snapping twigs pregnant with snakes and bears. Anyone who has spent a few nights out without getting killed, or gets tired enough, simply lets go. Those used to a good sleep in the wilds may eventually find their home mattress somehow ungiving after the undulations of bedrock, sand or soft soil.

No one has discovered for certain why most of us vertebrates need to sleep at all, though theories abound. By the use of electroencephalographs that monitor the brain waves of sleepers, we do know that the most restorative sleep alternates between periods of dreaming and periods of mental blankness. There is the sleep when we are participants in irrational fantasies, known as REM sleep for the rapid eye movement that accompanies it, and intervals when the brain takes a complete break. A camping trip—composed of days when life is vivid, unfamiliar and ego-diminished, and nights of sheer oblivion—extends that pattern over a period of days or weeks. Hallucination, blackout; hallucination, blackout: a wilderness trip extends the night's cycle to embrace the waking hours. It is at least teasing that campers back from a satisfying trip feel restored as if after sleep, on a grander scale. And they recall it in sleep's vocabulary.

One recent theory on the function of dreams, expressed by Carl Sagan in *The Dragons of Eden*, is that they give necessary expression to more primitive parts of our brains, developed when we were simpler forms of mammals, and reptiles before that. Our huge neo-cortex, whose cleverness and adaptability so distinguishes us from other animals, developed rapidly and has had little time to integrate itself with older parts of our psyche. Kept in check during the day by our dominant human consciousness, the instinctive parts of our brain need their own moments of expression, lest they erupt at the wrong time and drive us mad. Dreaming is thus a safety-vent for

The Telling Distance

impulses that no longer apply.

If Sagan is right, it may be that the urge to invade the wilds, where one can escape social pressure and wield a more intuitive kind of intelligence, is also related to the need to give expression to older parts of our psyche—a time, perhaps, when we were pre-civilized hunters, if not earlier mammals and reptiles. The wilderness ambushes us with sights and sensations that demand a quicker, keener kind of response. Abilities we didn't know we had come suddenly into play. The civilized person who meets a primitive demand, instead of feeling demeaned, may experience an unexpected elation. The greater the adventure, the more refreshed the camper is likely to feel afterward. A good camping trip and a dream-filled sleep, in quite different ways, both feel like acts of integration, connecting us with otherwise exiled parts of ourselves.

Bruce Berger

The human mind is perhaps more tangled than any wilderness we are trying to save, and has connections we are only beginning to make out. It may be that dreaming and wilderness travel are so invigorating because they form bridges to a past still within us, stranded in inaccessible parts of our being. That might explain why a journey to the wilds, with all its elements of chance, discomfort and strangeness, seems for so many like a homecoming, a return to something lost. It might also explain the alleged irrationality of wilderness defenders—and suggest why the need for wilderness, passionately felt, is so hard to articulate, and so crucial to our balance.

DESIGNER

DESERTS

Of Will and the Desert

M y mother's five acres of subdivided cactus outside
Phoenix is tended by an electronics student, a
veteran of Vietnam and a failed marriage, who gardens in
return for a room off the garage and a small stipend. Other
than pruning and studying computer circuitry, his only
activity is participation in a small Presbyterian church that
has split from the parent organization to protest the
ordaining of women and gays—fifty traditionalists struggling for an ecclesiastical identity. He maintains their
grounds as a devotion. Clean featured, heavy set, slow
moving, shy of eye contact, pleasant but devoid of humor,
Will's very blandness generates a certain mystery. My
mother recently remarked, "It doesn't seem healthy for a
man his age to spend that much time reading the Bible."

In an age of consumerism and the play ethic, Will is a
staunch throwback. "I just love to clean up," he says, "and
when I get going I just can't stop." Not a tare escapes.
Between poison, strong hands and the rake, only gravel
grows in the drive. Plants, potted or in beds, are watered
on time. The shrubs to either side of the door, whether
bottlebrush, privet or feathery cassia, are sheared to be
eggs on legs, greeting the guests like a panel of Jehovah's
Witnesses. The oleanders around the parking area, whose
tops undulated under the care of the late Mexican care-
taker, are straight as a cinderblock wall. It is as if grace
were the first step toward chaos.

All would be well if my mother's spread did not contain
two terrains and three sensibilities. The local homes,

strewn through five-acre zoning, are feigned oases, clusters of date palms, eucalyptus, silk oaks, pepper trees, locusts and other exotics that create a ferny air of secrecy. And all of them surround an actual body of water—the swimming pool—which is attached to a network of pipes that ultimately taps, and gradually depletes, the aquifer on which Paradise Valley sits. The habitation is typically a sprawling ranch-style house with Spanish touches: a tile portico, a wall of bougainvillea, an alcove with a mirror or an abstract Virgin. It is the Southwestern Dream: every man to his own waterhole.

The foliage around the houses is geometric in the rational tradition, but what gives the homes of Paradise Valley their special flavor—and status—is their setting in what's left of the Sonoran Desert. That setting is variously conceived. The Philistines simply bulldoze all that grows, then repair to a chic nursery to buy, at inflated prices, saguaros, Joshua trees, barrel cacti and prickly pear, many of which have been rustled from public lands. Stuck in clean raked yards, they resemble statues in a parking lot. The sophisticates not only leave the native vegetation; they supplement it with exotic cacti from Mexico and Argentina, along with a fashionable weeping palm known as *Coco plumosa* that requires vast amounts of water and invariably dies, draping the neighborhood with sad brown fountains. Once the eye has adjusted to the way cactus space themselves in unimproved desert, the supplemental effect is as grotesque as the sculptured parking lot, and philosophically on a par with a solipsist society.

Everyone may have a landscape of the heart—not necessarily one's birthplace, but a terrain that corresponds to some inner spring. Mine is the Sonoran Desert, which I first saw as a small child in the late forties, only a few miles from my mother's present home. At that time there were unbroken stands of saguaros bustling with jackrabbits, roadrunners, coyotes, chuckawallas, doves and quail, all the cackling, shrieking, chuckling and hooting creatures

Bruce Berger

of a raucous ecosystem. So many odd, independent selves woven into so strident a harmony made me race from one oddity to the next, lest some marvel escape. Over the years I have managed to return from time to time, to touch base even when life led me elsewhere. So now it is like a homecoming, three decades after the first visit, to rent my house in the mountains during the winter and share the oasis left to my mother by the Arizonan she married. I play the absentee landlord in the landscape that feels like home.

For years the grounds were maintained by a genial and plant-loving Mexican who lived by the garage. Aging, plagued by numerous ailments, José allowed vegetation to grow to its natural contours, trimmed off the excess, then escaped the body's limits in a folding armchair, dreaming in the sun. When José's arthritis got too painful I took over watering the *Cocos plumosa,* postponing their demise while I admired the vitality around them. During the six years of José's tenure I fell in love with my mother's scrap of the desert, and took its continuity for granted. The roadrunners had disappeared, the horizon was blurred with smog and the air tortured by helicopters, but three kinds of woodpeckers still nested in the saguaros. The oleanders were two-story apartments, with house finches above and Gambel quail below. Hawks floated overhead, then dropped to the neighbors' eucalyptus. Coyotes squabbled at night, cottontails hid among the creosote bushes and dawn turned the jackrabbits' ears to shells of coral. One season a screech owl moved into a hole in a saguaro and spent his days like José, sunning his face with his eyes closed. It was luxurious to set up the typewriter on a card table by the house's neglected south end, a corner sealed by oleanders, creosote bushes and a palo verde full of birds, and let my senses wander when inspiration failed. Pierced by planes, distant construction and the bop of a nearby tennis court, it was less neutral than Proust's cork-lined room, but it ventilated the spirit.

For years the desert flourished under José's benign

The
Telling
Distance

neglect. Then my mother's husband died, and José, as if loyal beyond the grave, soon followed. With the oasis pared to two inhabitants, and my own summer absence impending, it was obvious that José had to be replaced—for safety as well as for maintenance. Paradise Valley, like everything in the desert, has its predator, a species of house thief who adapts as security systems evolve, who strikes at night, or in the owner's absence, or in his presence to his own peril. Alarms, usually set off by mistake, outwail the coyotes. Meanwhile, I was the substitute José. It was more intricate than I thought, figuring how much water each plant needed, or even how water reached it, but there was great peace in it. The desert, after a wet winter, had never been so lush. That spring a hummingbird built a nest just outside the living room window: a little straw jewel box just four inches from the glass where mama incubated like the lid on a doll's casserole. I never felt closer to miracle.

Bruce
Berger

In the limbo of that spring we made separate travel plans: myself for a May backpack, my mother for a June trip east. The house would stand empty only a day. For two weeks, while Utah slickrock soared over my head, I dreamt of my month alone with the creatures of suburban Phoenix. It was not the sense of proprietorship, but of being the sole consciousness among so many treasured lives—of watching them day by day unwatched by my own kind. I saw myself having morning coffee among the saguaros, typing in the buff at my secret card table, sipping scotch while the late sun turned the McDowell Mountains to ripples of red silk.

When we climbed out of the canyons a day early I called collect, hoping to catch my mother before she left. A stranger accepted the call. "Your mother left this morning," he said in an elusive drawl.

"And who is this?"

"Will. Your mother hired me to look after the place."

I drove back to Phoenix in a cool, detached fury.

By June, Phoenix middays are too scalding even for

lizards and the desert steeps in silence, but Will was hot at work, pulling the weeds I had secretly spared. I spied from windows, nervous, angry, vengeful, keeping track of the latest. Hoses ran, hedge clippers keened, flower beds were reduced to petunias and dirt, as a transistor tuned to soft rock followed Will around. My blood rebelled the more I saw the irony—that he was simply following orders, making up for my own indulgence, diligently and in the heat. I had feelings; he had instructions. It was when I heard Debbie Boone moaning halfway down the drive, out in the desert, in *my* terrain, that my blood boiled over. The two-wheeled track that had given one the sense of reaching the house, however briefly, through the wild, was being weeded into a suburban drive. Perhaps this was the first step in some rabid scheme to achieve the statue-in-parking-lot effect. We would be Philistines yet. "What are you doing out this far?" I asked, hearing my tension sound falsely off-hand.

"Just pulling weeds. Your mother told me to clean off the drive," he said, smiling and looking a little to the side.

"She must have meant the parking area. This part here was always meant to look natural."

"Well I have orders to weed the drive."

"These may look like weeds," I said, improvising in the strain of the moment, "but they're bursage, a native plant and part of the system. Jackrabbits need them for food and the quail need them for cover. Maybe you should wait until my mother gets back to make sure."

Amiably enough he loaded the spade in the wheelbarrow and followed me back up the drive.

Meanwhile mama hummingbird had fledged and two bills like hatpins poked from the nest. I watched through binoculars from the far end of the living room as mama zoomed out of sight, then shot back to their upturned bills. Will could be seen on the far side of the patio with the watercan. I ambled out. "Will, there are hummingbirds nesting in the atrium, right by the window, so you might watch out for them." He looked at me blankly. An hour later he climbed into the atrium with the watercan, huge among the ferny exotics, and to eyes tuned to humming-birds he resembled the arrival of the puppeteer. Mama was off getting food, and suddenly the two little ones rocketed from the nest and vanished forever. I felt like an abandoned parent. It is the nature of hummingbirds to leave the nest without flight instruction, but whether these were prepared I never knew. Soon afterward the bush was clipped and the nest itself disappeared.

Harder to accept than specific measures was the sense of a regimental consciousness interpreting orders during my reign of solitude. For Will's fervor implied more than a job; he was reforming the wilderness. When I wandered out in the morning with coffee, or in the evening with scotch, I felt his sober eyes upon me. Since life had zoned us in the same five acres, I felt I should ease communica-tion, and learned, as he spoke with his half-apologetic smile, gazing slightly off-center, that his great interest was in returning Presbyterianism to its true path. If he was personally critical he kept it to himself, and the real judgment, I realized, was the one I projected upon him. But the Sonoran Desert had been tuning itself to drought since the Pleistocene: compared with which even John Calvin was born yesterday. Why couldn't he just run the hose, then sun himself in a chair like José? His very attitude made war on the fabric I had hoped to merge with.

The next winter the roses were exhausted, needed new dirt, and there was nowhere to haul out the old dirt but through my secret corner. The oleanders were cut back to provide passage, a truck to bring the new soil sank permanent ruts through the soft winter ground, and the old dirt was spilled in a dead grey pile over some native grass. There was no other way to engineer the new rose garden, so I held my tongue. Then I heard a lawn mower snarling from the same direction, and found the vegeta-tion being gratuitously mowed beneath the palo verde.

"This is my office," I said, trying to sound practical and hearing it come out ridiculous, "and I need as much protection as possible. Please leave this corner the way it is."

"I was just trying to make it easier to get around," protested Will. "It's a good thing you stopped me in time. I'd have cut it all."

Then where does the third sensibility, the one nominally in charge, stand in all this? My mother wants to see the place well maintained, looking good, holding its own. She too loves the desert—but in general rather than in detail. It is a moody foreground for painterly effects of light, of mountain and sky, as well as a romantic setting for a house, to be spruced up, perhaps, with a few *Cocos plumosa*. But her real interest is the oasis: the shrubs, the flower beds, the drive, the atrium, the pool, the patio and its furniture. For that she needs help. The oleanders might be more sensitively curved, the cassias more flowing, but in the nineteen-eighties, with every value falling apart, Will is a genuine find. He is honest, quiet, irreplaceable: a Protestant José.

It is when Will's mission to straighten the oasis spills into the desert, my sacred chaos, that my own thoughts begin to transgress. The urge to tidy up nature and to prune humanity seem suddenly functions of the same calling. Freud's theories on obsessive cleanliness as self-avoidance make new sense. Phrases like anal compulsive swim to mind, and I think cynically of the acres of God's desert bulldozed into church parking lots. Letting resentment run, I think how it is the fate of those who love things as they grow—not to mention reclusive writers—to fit themselves into the gaps between noisier, blunter lives, where they are gradually squeezed out. The land may be indifferent, but we invest it with our feelings, then feel each loss like a personal amputation. Yet it is impossible to remain angry with a stolidity like Will's. Politeness, quietude, remoteness, even the vulnerability of averted eyes,

The Telling Distance

have an integrity our cheap demolishing age lacks.

And his very blandness is capable of surprise. I recently spotted his pickup halfway down the drive, heard Debbie Boone singing through the cactus, and rushed to fend off the latest assault. A saguaro, having rotted from age, had been toppled by a windstorm, and there was Will, pushing and groaning, planting a living arm in freshly turned earth and propping it up with boards. Saguaro limbs, unlike ivy clippings, will not send out new roots. But how could I tell Will his effort was doomed? "Here's another cactus for your desert," he said, smiling and looking to the side.

Bruce
Berger

The Dismantling

A notice from the building inspector greeted my mother's and my return to her house in suburban Phoenix. The loose aluminum roof on the shed in the back of the property constituted a serious safety hazard: would we call his office within five days and inform him of our plans to repair or remove the offending roof.

The shed, in fact, was a four-stall stable with wooden troughs, a couple of tiny enclosed rooms for tack, and a small fenced paddock for each horse. It had been installed by the house's builders in the late fifties, when the neighborhood was horsey, residents left the cactus standing, and homes were romantic desert hideaways. The five-acre zoning remained in effect, but newer residents incorporated the Great Indoors, covered most of the lot with the house itself, cleared off the messy vegetation, and left a few token saguaros or barrel cactus like toys in a sandbox. Older homes nearby had stables so nearly like ours one suspected the same hand at construction, but their aluminum siding roofs had been sensibly weighted with rocks. Half of our aluminum had already blown off and glittered about the shed like fallen petals. The rest lifted in the slightest breeze and rattled like stage thunder. If neighbors objected, perhaps they were put out that every desert storm sounded like a high school production of *The Tempest.*

My mother's first question to the inspector was whether someone had complained. No, the inspector merely happened to be checking upon construction of a new brick palazzo, heard an odd rattling, and noticed all that aluminum just ready to sail. A stiff wind might wing a sheet of metal straight into a stray schoolchild. In three decades none of the silver petals had migrated more than a quarter of the distance to the fence, and it was hard to imagine one bothering more than a jackrabbit. But my mother, ignoring that neighbors had duplicates of our own shed, protested that the building was an eyesore and an embarrassment, and promised to have the entire structure pulled down at the first opportunity.

A recurrent dream: I am walking through a house where I am a guest, and stumble upon a secret room. Or it is a house where I have lived many years—years invented by the dream—and a hitherto unnoticed door gives way to secret stairs that climb to an attic, or descend to a basement room where a couple of frosted windows at ground level leak daylight. I'm feverish to explore everything at once, for the room is crammed with stuffed birds and fish, tapestries, stacked oil paintings, boxes with sliding panels that give way to old coins, lacquered desks, geodes, tinted postcards, cobalt glassware, parchment lamps, maps of further secret places. If I wake during my prowl or, worse, am wakened, I panic and grab for the nearest object so that I may surface with, say the pearl-handled opera glasses in my hand . . .

Given an obsession with secret places, one would think I had explored the shed's last recess. I had, to be sure, stuck my head in its spaces and had a general idea of the contents, but the dreams of secret rooms, laced with the odd cobweb, talcumed with dust, never confronted shredded cardboard and asbestos, snarled wire, heaped packing material, undifferentiated grey litter, and habitat for the black widow that deepened with every step toward the interior. Now that we were about to lose it, I forced myself to take inventory: a collapsed wheelchair, a typewriter with no moving parts, cushions lost in their stuffing, a decorative iron grille, a couch with erupting upholstery, a pot lid collection, a dresser the hue of skin-colored bandaids, a badminton net, a bleached ice bucket, a fire extinguisher, petrified rubber boots, a chaise longue painted blue and, incredibly, one quite edible looking bale of hay. The chaise longue, in its original bamboo, graced the porch of the house where I grew up, and the grille had once subdivided an apartment my mother kept in Chicago. The provenance of the hay was clear. Wherever the rest came from, one wouldn't care to wake with any of it in one's hands.

The actual treasure was on the outside; it was the building. Below the quivering roof the wood had weathered into sweeps of mahogany, auburn, chocolate, sepia, an entire palette from charcoal to ash, tide-rippled with grain, eyelit with knotholes. Desert grasses in the paddocks, in northern shade, grew dense and lush. The back side, which received the runoff from the shed roof, was deep in palo verdes, and at one corner stood a monumental clump of Engelmann prickly pear whose wax yellow roses, blooming each May against the shed's patina, just cried for their Sunday painter. For all its regrettable contents the building was long, dark, heavily vegetated, a heap of mystery and shadow. Less than a candidate for the National Register, it evoked a time within middle-aged memory when people in Phoenix still played at living in the West. If the contents were emptied, the aluminum stripped, the wood left standing . . . No; it was an embarrassment; it had to go.

To make sure there was nothing to salvage I made one more tour of the interior. Stepping gingerly through the tack room rubble I looked around, and back. Obscured by the door I'd pushed open, the very grey of oblivion, stood a previously unseen four-drawer filing cabinet. After minor tugging all four drawers pulled open, and all four were filled with papers. One was stuffed with unused letter paper and envelopes from a Chicago insurance company, a lifetime supply of the wrong stationery. Another was full of tax records. A third contained bulging manila envelopes full of sorted greeting cards. One envelope disgorged what must have been all the get-well cards received during the lifetime of one person, surely an invalid. There was an envelope of birthday cards, of St. Patrick's Day cards, of Easter cards. Occasional canceled stamps dated them from the forties and fifties, and almost every card, whatever the event, featured cute animals in a dated style. Christmas, which might have overwhelmed the stable, was absent.

It was the drawer I'd saved for last that consumed the afternoon. Here was the record of two lifetimes, and documents of countless more. The letters, loose, in folders, even tied with ribbons, were hard to decipher, and I pried in snatches. He was constantly on the road, loved her more than anything else in the world, repeatedly begged her forgiveness, and swore to do better. She was always finding novel topics for the garden club, and was making good progress thanks to AA. He left an envelope of letters to the editor about Chicago politics; she left some pressed poppies still tinged with yellow, folded into a paper that was inscribed, apparently in Arizona, "Gathered along the road on New Years Day, 1934." There were photos of dozens of weddings, graduations, excursions, and babies—one baby or a dozen babies?—alike as newborn harp seals. His death preceded hers. She left her will: nothing should go to her foster parents; all went to a female friend. Those people, I realized, were the brother and sister-in-law of my mother's late husband, the Arizonan she married years after the death of my father. And by the end of the afternoon I felt emotionally drained, not so much by the pathos of these individual lives as by this jumble of process itself, of death, recrimination, apology, birth, illness, devotion, recreation, and the desperate attempt to hold on, to save, to file away, to stop the headlong rush to whatever came next. Whatever else you could say for it, this cycle we are all forced to go through is simply exhausting.

And someone should have the opportunity, even at this

late date, to stop the show. I called my mother's late husband's granddaughter, the one descendant who lived in the Valley. She arrived displaying the station wagon they'd just bought, and chattered to my mother about her children's new outfits. She followed gamely in her spotless clothes through the cactus to the stable, peered in with little comment, then looked at a few treasures I'd set aside in case she didn't want to go through it all. Yes, she knew who these people were. But who would want to plow through all this stuff now? Not her relatives, and certainly not her. This sorority diary with the old snapshots was kind of interesting, she'd take that. And further enlarging on the new playsuits she left with her souvenir.

But a few of the less personal items might still be of interest, and I contacted Goodwill. To my horror they showed up with a van vast enough to gut Hearst Castle and which waited outside the fence as two elderly gentlemen looked at the building from the outside with unconcealed disgust. Everything was open to the weather? No, I assured them, there were two enclosed rooms, please look. I led them to where the dresser sat in perfect condition except for the peeling top. Didn't they employ disabled persons to restore such items? Surely I'd seen on the local news . . . No, they didn't hire the handicapped. But what about this badminton net? They accepted it. They accepted the pot lids. What about this iron grille? The fire extinguisher? The wheelchair? No, they said without explanation, climbed into their truck and backed away.

Finally there was the wood, the kind of wood I'd seen used for paneling in homes and restaurants, for framing, for rustic improvisations. And here we came to the technicality that the buildings on the property, as opposed to their contents, were not my mother's. They were hers to use during her lifetime, then passed to her late husband's heirs, and meanwhile were managed by the Bank. The Bank would pay for the shed's demolition, and the Bank would choose the demolisher after bids had been made. Two demolishers soon appeared, and the first, to my surprise, was quite ecstatic over the wood. It was really beautiful, and there was a great market for it on the West Coast. So what about Phoenix? He'd check. The iron grille was also interesting. I showed him the files of papers, and he remarked that someone absolutely should construct a genealogy of these people. Greeting card buffs would love these cards, they would fill gaps in collections. Someone should go through the stamps . . . Here was someone possibly more obsessed with salvation than myself; collaboration might actually be a joy.

The second wreckers closely resembled the men from Goodwill. I pointed out the beauty of the wood, and asked about its possible salvage. Well, it might make a few picture frames, but the labor of pulling it apart by hand without injuring it would far outweigh its commercial value. Were there any snakes? Every couple of years I'd seen a king snake in the garden, but none around the shed, nor any rattlers on the property. Fine, they'd do a good job of hauling it out. They underbid the first demolisher by a factor of three and were hired by the Bank.

Soon afterward we met to discuss routes of egress. They'd take things out the back to make the least disturbance. That's where the best vegetation was, I said, and led them around. They agreed; instead they'd bring the stable through one of the stalls, making it sound like pulling a sweater inside out. But they might have to disturb a couple of those little bushes. That's all right, my mother assured them, there were lots of them. I shot her a look. As soon as the men were gone I reminded her that we were talking about the bush that had saved her life.

That was chaparral?

That was creosote, the plant chaparral was made from. Some twenty years back my mother had contracted a disease called lupus, for which there is no known cure and which took, among others, the writer Flannery O'Connor.

Bruce
Berger

She got what treatments were available from a specialist in Chicago, and several years later, for wholly unrelated reasons, started taking an herb called chaparral. Within two days the lupus disappeared. Several years later she had a slight recurrence, resumed the chaparral, and the lupus again vanished. At that point she informed her old doctor in Chicago, who assured her it was just coincidence and of no consequence medically. The herb's name is a misnomer, for the word "chaparral" refers to a life zone well above the Lower Sonoran, where creosote grows—nor does the herb's label mention anything so grand as a cure for lupus. But certain rings of the creosote are now believed to be earth's oldest living inhabitants, older than the sequoia, older than the bristlecone. While we were innate consumers, not much oriented toward honoring the life forms that sustain us, I felt we owed a certain debt toward the creosote. Besides, tell a contractor he can nick one bush and he'll mash fifteen.

It was with misgivings that I greeted the crew of three that showed up the first morning of the dismantling. They were not interested in even the mildest conversation about the heat and I left them alone, hoping for the best. There was no whine of machinery, only occasional banging and the skreak of nails being pulled out. At the end of the day I saw daylight through the back of the shed, and undamaged boards lay neatly stacked. The building came down by a process of quiet subtraction. Gone was the perilous aluminum siding. Gone were the Vesuvial sofa, the dresser, the chaise longue, the iron grille. Then there was the grey filing cabinet. Its arrangers of letters, photos, and holiday greetings—how valiantly they'd tried to interest the future. Of no concern to their descendants, draining my patience in an afternoon, could they really persuade me to find history in their obsessions and homes for their cute cards? I seldom saved cards, myself, but have stored, in alphabetical files, almost every letter I have ever received. From what stable would my own life vanish? I kidded myself by retrieving the poppies and a few stamps, but gone, too, was the grey filing cabinet.

At the end of the third day I wandered out to find an astonishing sight: the old wheelchair, unfolded, stood alone in the desert facing what remained of a cock-eyed wooden frame, a couple of paddocks, and a strip of bare ground ending in trees and sky. Another pile of unmarred and stacked brown boards waited to be hauled away. Hadn't they actually taken the stable down in the careful, labor intensive manner they said was so prohibitive? Had they deliberately underbid the other fellow because they planned to make money off the material all along? Were they salvaging the wood and cheating the Bank? I could only hope so.

By the end of the fourth day it was as if the shed had been conjured off the spot. There was a rectangle of bare earth, interrupted by a slab of cement where the tack rooms had been. The palo verdes behind the shed revealed a strange configuration, having grown uniformly away from the building, then branched over the roof so that each contained the same tipped, right-angled cutout, giving this roundish tree a look of wind-blown cypress. The prickly pear pads were jaundiced where they had abutted the building, and would green up or fall off. Cactus and trees could now expand to their normal shapes, but would they luxuriate without the contorting roof to deliver them water? The creosote had apparently wielded their survival powers, for they had watched an entire building pass without injury.

These swaying palo verdes and the slab of concrete suddenly suggested subdued lighting and a dance floor, and it struck me that the shed was a storehouse of associations—of material, documentation, possession, past lives and a passed way of life—awaiting condemnation to make themselves known. But for the bale of hay the building might never have seen a horse, and been intended as a halfway house for things no longer useful but too laden to throw away. They had years, decades of grace. Then without warning these bits of matter and memory simultaneously passed the angle of repose and started hurtling, unstoppable, toward wherever things finally disappear.

Meanwhile the desert had a new stretch of bare ground to work with. What would lay claim? That would be worth watching.

The
Telling
Distance

The Assault of Squaw Peak

Bruce Berger

Squaw Peak, on the fringes of downtown Phoenix, is the kind of slag heap most mountaineers, not to mention other mountains, look down on. Behind a tract of ranchettes off a crosstown artery, Squaw Peak Park is the crown of the Phoenix City Park System. From a basin of picnic ramadas, johns and trash barrels, its shaggy pyramid rises twelve hundred feet above the valley floor, bearing a populous trail of switchbacks, traverses and last scrambles that winds a mile from the parking lot to the city's beloved summit. Once a mere granite outcropping, Squaw Peak has become that contemporary urban phenomenon, an exercise mountain. It is simultaneously a social club, a point of reference, a spiritual escape, a vertical dog walk, a unit of measurement, a free place to lose weight, a training ground, an addiction, and to its more passionate admirers—and I am one—the focus of a most curious subculture.

My introduction to Squaw Peak occurred on one of those days of blustery smog that passes for winter in Phoenix. On reaching the summit I came upon six adults speaking a tongue I couldn't identify. Teutonic gutturals, Gallic nasals, Balkan clots of consonants, it seemed to confound all of Europe. I selected its most American-looking practitioner and asked. "A dialect of Swiss," the lady replied, "native to only a few cantons. I'm not very good at it myself yet. I'm from Chicago and only recently married into it." Through that linguistic scramble came a clear message from Squaw Peak itself: its glory was its people.

Motives for scaling Squaw Peak are various. A few couples are less interested in the ascent than in some amorphous rock to crawl behind for a roll in the cactus. A few first-timers hope to commune with nature. There are various one-shot groups: geology classes, Scout troops, outing clubs, gangs, church picnics. Some are looking for a comfortable perch where they can let Phoenix go nonverbal; others arrive with the problems of the world transistorized in their hands. But the regulars are there for exercise. Imagine yourself on the summit as a woman in a pink tank shirt and tennis shorts lurches to the top rock, flops down and looks immediately at her watch. "Damn! Twenty minutes and seventeen seconds."

A man in a sweat suit who has watched her last pitch says, "Still haven't broken the twenty-minute barrier?"

"Yeah, but I don't think I can ever do better than this. Cloudy day, Reeboks. Not much better than with hiking boots in the sun. What's your best time?"

"Twenty-two-oh-five. You beat *me,* in any case."

As they split seconds an enormous hulk of a regular, minus his usual overweight companion, flings himself on a neighboring rock and squints at a stopwatch. "Finally did it," he gasps. "Took me two months, but I broke twenty-six minutes."

"Congratulations!" says the man.

"Great," says the woman, "but where's your friend?"

"We can't seem to get our schedules together anymore," he sighs. "Tuesdays and Thursdays I go to the Trim 'n Slim to use the pool, and he goes bowling on Mondays, plays bingo on Wednesdays and sees his mother on Friday. We run into each other on weekends sometimes and he says, 'See you on Tuesday and Thursday?' and I say, 'See you on Monday, Wednesday and Friday?' It's hopeless."

While the trio ponders life's unfairness, a late adolescent in yellow shorts, sleek as a Pentecostal, bounds to the top, grunts a general salutation and disappears back down.

He makes two round trips every afternoon, never slowing to speak, always in the same yellow shorts as supernaturally spotless as John Wayne's hat. Does he have more than one pair? Wash them everyday? Possess a divine detergent? If you know every turn, your brain needs such roughage.

Squaw Peak is no less valuable to equipment testers. It is possible, when school is out, to observe a group of subteens and their adult counselor all with shiny new red and white packs from a backpack emporium known locally as High Indenture. Affixed to each pack is a sleeping bag projected backward to apply maximum stress to the bearer's spine. The sleeping bag of one little boy dangles from his frame's bottom corner so that it swings wildly, pulling him like a sad pendulum in its wake. More sophisticated testers climb with their packs empty, adding weights to the outside until they attain back-country poundage. And Squaw Peak is not forgotten once its graduates hit the trail; drilled into bone memory, it becomes a unit of measurement. The Grand Canyon is four Squaw Peaks. The Grand Teton is five and a half. Mt. Everest is twenty-two.

There is, of course, the doggy set. As a breed fancier I enjoy the variety, the counterpoint with their owners, the aromatic pitfalls that await the sprint back down. Most heroic is a toy poodle whose mistress marches it daily to the summit. It is a sweating dog's fate to look happier the hotter it gets, but this creature seems truly delighted; under all that fluff must crouch a little rat of sheer muscle. More elegant was an afghan I once found rounding the bends alone with melancholy determination, hair blowing in the wind. He remained mysterious for several turns, until I came upon an emaciated young man with an aquiline nose and streaming blond locks, who couldn't figure what was so hilarious when he said hello.

Casual encounters can resonate with meaning. Once at the summit I came upon a pack of Marlboros with each cigarette angrily broken in half and strewn about the empty pack—an oath in litter to live more purely. I came once upon a couple bearing two children, a two-year-old riding a seat on his back, an infant slung on her stomach and contentedly sucking her left breast as she climbed. I have seen kids huffing up the trail on clunker bikes, and one late teen staggering up with a fifteen-pound rock in his arms. In the parking lot on a day of driving rain I was asked by a heavy-set fellow in sopping track shorts, barely slowing up, whether I had seen signs of lightning on top. "I'm out to make a record," he panted. "On my eighth lap. I'll quit after ten or an even dozen. Don't know if it's the mountain's record. It's mine. The most I've gone before is 9,000 feet. At 9,700 now. That's two Grand Canyons." And one dusk I came upon three Native Americans in track suits at a leveling of the trail, jogging in a tight circle. Muscle warm-up? Mystic rite? Two birds with one stone? Squaw Peak holds its tongue . . .

Squaw Peak on weekends is a sociological dare. The slopes are alive with children unleashing aggressions built up from five consecutive days of public education, and many of them are throwing rocks. You dodge your way to the summit between cousinly gangs and downhill sprinters. On the summit you try to stay out of victory photographs, then a young voice yells to another, "Don't go yet, John, I've got to get my recorder out of your pack!" You perk up, hoping someone will blow a few bars of Scarlatti, but no, a young hand brandishes a tape deck. The sign below must be incomplete: this must be Squawk Peak. There is nothing left but to sprint back down like Nureyev the Coyote, speed-reading T-shirts, dodging dog duty, slaloming through scout troops, family picnics, beer and dope and hot dog parties, ignoring rolling rocks, amateur police whistles and the top ten, until you can unlock your car door and fasten the safety belt.

If Squaw Peak is romantic, it is only at night. In a metropolis like Phoenix, bristling with arc lights, neon lights and headlights, a shimmering twilight reigns from dusk until dawn and the trail glows like a radium dial. Few brave the mountain, and fellow hikers pass like phantoms. I have risked it occasionally, most unforgettably one night before Christmas. An unfamiliar voice sounded, *Uh-ooh-ooh-ooh!* I feared at first a clever mugger, but safe passage proved it a true owl. Christmas lights on the eaves of ranchettes crawled like coral snakes through the dark. Such night ascents prolong short winter days and extend the exercise season through the hot months, but I don't attempt Squaw Peak very often after sundown. I am not afraid of the trail, but I am terrified of the parking lot.

A friend of mine who grew up at the base of Squaw Peak remembers when a trip to the summit from his house was an all-day affair. That was before motorized access made it the mountain for the man on the go. Since then it has been discovered that exercise can stave off atrophy and fat attacks, and ease the pressures of junk food, blush wines and Blue Cross payments. The hordes have arrived, devout consumers, and they believe that the only route is straight up. Switchbacks are shaved, ignored, obliterated. Whole pitches become alleys, then avenues. The more adventurous find the trail demeaning and select some nearly perpendicular alternative, launching everything loose. Rockslides become gullies, gullies become gashes, the vegetation gives up and the mountain becomes a chronic landslide. The City Park System in collaboration with volunteers has valiantly outlined the trail with rocks, strewn rubble over the cut-offs, jockeyed steps, added strategic handrails and even reared retaining walls, retarding wholesale collapse. Still, parts of Squaw Peak aren't eroding so much as they are melting like ice cream.

My affection for Squaw Peak is colored by one private association: my mother married the Arizonan who owned the undeveloped valley in back of it, just under the peak, a square mile known as Section 36. Acquired in the forties, it was once a peaceful domain where a gentleman could pull up his Lincoln and let out his poodles. Trail bikes changed all that. Signs prohibiting all but foot traffic were

Bruce Berger

posted, adding the lure of the forbidden to young Knievels pioneering new ruts through the arroyos, until Section 36 sang like a swarm of electronic mosquitos. Meanwhile city taxes were spiraling, revenues held their own at zero and Frank Durham was being broken by Squaw Peak.

Developers offered lurid sums for the privilege of turning Section 36 into fully secured townhouses with pools and golf course, but Frank held out for cactus. I played my single card by calling Nature Conservancy in Tucson, hoping they might intervene; there followed a silence in which I imagined incredulity at anything in Phoenix worth conserving, then an explanation that they had sunk all their funds into something outside Tucson called Rancho Romero. Suddenly my stepfather ran across a newspaper photo of Mayor Driggs and associates riding through Section 36 on horseback, hoping to annex it to the open space program. With his usual flair Frank called City Hall, got Mayor Driggs on his line and growled, "What do you mean by trespassing on my land?" There followed two years of negotiations in which Section 36 was sold to the city for a fraction of its market value. Frank Durham joined the Driggs for Governor Committee, and the back of Squaw Peak, refenced, was saved as an urban refuge.

And Squaw Peak, beckoning darkly between downtown skyscrapers, still offers the consolations of perspective. Those consolations are necessary. Sirens howl through Phoenix like wolves all night. City cherry pickers armed with chain saws tidy the palms by day. Mowers, hedge clippers and radios keen to each other from back yards. Dobermans and yappers debate the alleys. Peace in the city seems to consist in drowning out your neighbor with the havoc of your choice, but from the summit of Squaw Peak the voices run together in one pure stereophonic roar. Only the pitched combustion of a plane or the sine wave of a police car can pick itself from the din, to lapse back into chaos. It is a fugue for a million voices, and if you lie back with your eyes closed you can almost feel all that energy, and even dream yourself—if you dare—its final product.

You reopen your eyes to find Western civilization splintering in all directions. On many days it is hard to see beyond Sun City, and one of the ironies of Squaw Peak is that its horizons, once achingly pure, have blurred and vanished until you wonder whether you are building your legs only to rot your lungs. But say a clean wind has blown in from Los Angeles. Toward the horizon in diminishing waves of blue stretch the mountains: the Superstitions, the McDowells, Sierra Estrella, the South Mountains, Four Peaks, the Mazatzals, more ranges than you can name. At their feet lies the tawny lionskin of the Sonoran Desert, whose cactus still keep their spines out and drink alone. And like a house pet nearby lies the better-known Camelback Mountain, also an exercise mountain but so barbed with electroguarded homes that few commoners have found the trail up its exclusive hump.

Bruce Berger

Just out of sight at the end of the McDowells, a splinter in the mind's eye, stands an improbable shaft of white. Courtesy of McCulloch Properties, the folks who brought us the London Bridge, it is the world's tallest fountain, an ejaculation of pure ground water. Collected over the centuries in a vast aquifer that underlies this particular waste, it attains its consummation in one clean upward rush into the dry Sonoran air, thence to evaporate. Its mission is not the irrigation of life but the promotion of real estate. Into this waste an inverted Wall of China called the Central Arizona Project has been constructed to divert, for four billion tax dollars, what's left of the Colorado River—but if we get lost in the Arizona mind we will never make it off this mountain.

More immediately, great quadrangles of asphalt and green are still spreading their dazzling geometry in all directions, a few of them, like the saturated McCormick Ranch, bent on outdoing Connecticut. High rises compound the sub-centers of Tempe and Scottsdale. The better homes cantilever their egos into the public eye on steep hillsides, spilling prize desert into simulated mine dumps. What's left of the Salt River Valley, assisted by the Mafia, the real estate lobby and the Congressional delegation, is swiftly being paved or bulldozed into dervishes of liberated topsoil. *Ave atque valley.*

Yet stand on Squaw Peak, chance a deep breath, and gaze. You are at the hub of a great wheel, and flashing about you are the accelerating spokes of the New West. They may look raw. But in the heart of the true Phoenician, the newcomer or the native of a decade's standing, lies the faith, the fountain, the drive of Phoenix's founding myth, that from the recurrent ashes of itself will continue to flame the eternally new pigeon.

The
Telling
Distance

The Designer Deserts of Greater Phoenix

In a letter published by *Arizona Highways* in May, 1940, Frank Lloyd Wright offered southern Arizona some advice. A true civilization could grow around Phoenix, but only if it abstracted the desert's own patterns, broke the light with its own forms, fused with what the desert already possessed. The cactus forests, the leopard-spotted mountains, and pure desert air comprised a garden unequalled in the rest of the world, and no crop could be as precious, even economically, as the cactus visitors would travel hundreds of miles to see. Arizonans must beware of the "candy-makers and cactus-hunters" who would develop the desert until it was gone.

Such reading is quaint—and a little heart-breaking—to those who have watched the Phoenix scenario unravel. Founded in 1867 on the site of an ancient Hohokam village, by the time of Wright's arrival in 1928 Phoenix had become a lively desert oasis, compact, Spanish-American in flavor. While the rest of the country wrestled with the ensuing Depression, Phoenix thrived by encouraging the rich to wear blue jeans and attend chuck wagons at exclusive dude ranches. Governor Hunt convened his government in a soiled white suit in the shade of the capitol lawn, exposed to all constituents. Wright, reborn as a desert prophet, would swoop in from his architectural school out in the cactus, ordering clerks about in his black cape and broad-brimmed hat, and instructing waitresses to seat his entourage at the most visible table in the center of the room. The few restaurants that required coats and

Bruce
Berger

ties issued them at the door, and locals complained of the heat less than they boasted of ways to beat it. They survived by keeping windows closed, blinds drawn, ceiling fans revolving, and winter rugs rolled up so that bare feet could touch wood or cool cement. Canvas awnings were lowered over windows at dawn, and vine-covered verandas were hosed for an evaporative cooling effect—a trick so old it was called "the way Cleopatra kept cool." Most houses had screened-in porches known as "Arizona rooms," or gazebos where families socialized in the evenings and then went to sleep on cots in perfect safety. Phoenicians wore hats with moistened inner bands, carried umbrellas, did not attempt suntans, and knew what we have forgotten: that it is hot drinks rather than iced ones that cool you off. If anyone braved the summer sun for reasons other than work, it was to be pulled on a surfboard through the irrigation canals, holding a rope from a car.

It was just after Wright's blast to *Arizona Highways* that Phoenix's golden age was broken in upon by World War II and air conditioning. Phoenix was suddenly annexed by the Air Force. American and British pilots trained in the area, companies like Sperry-Rand made aviation equipment, and local cotton fields turned out silk for parachutes. There were detention camps for German prisoners of war, and supervised crews of prisoners did street work and garbage detail. All Phoenix became a kind of extended military base, and the U. S. Government poured sums of money into digging wells, paving and lighting streets, and initiating flood control to protect their airfields. The Mafia first arrived at that time, drawn by the infusion of bucks.

It was also the federal government that developed air conditioning in a big way. Minor use of the evaporative or "swamp" cooler actually preceded the war, and was even invented locally; what the military brought in was full-fledged air conditioning, or refrigeration. Natives were so enthusiastic that many at first slept right in front of the unit and got pneumonia. The expense of air conditioning fell as it became popular, and its long range effect was to make Phoenix habitable all year even for those who couldn't take the heat, since one's house became a micro-climate, adjustable at will.

Many who spent the war in Phoenix, cooled by federal air conditioning, stayed on or returned, and proof of the area's magnetism is that even German prisoners came back and lost themselves as best they could in the social fabric. But when the chic new hostelries and exclusive shops grew up on the city's fringes, Phoenix succumbed. One survivor dates the death of downtown at the installation of parking meters, which so enraged locals that they fled to new shopping centers rather than feed a machine. Another blames the end of the trolley system. Old buildings were felled with such indifference that Phoenix is now accused of having "a tradition of no tradition." Visitors lured by the city's reputation found themselves engulfed by asphalt, street signs and doomed businesses, and moved to resorts further out. Phoenix became one more city modeled on the grass fire, crackling at the edges and burning out in the center.

Bruce
Berger

Now that a half-century of refrigeration has eliminated the need to adapt, what has become of Wright's notion that a civilization could grow around Phoenix by merging with what the desert already possessed? At first it would seem that the idea was simply dismissed. Today's developer typically begins by bulldozing everything on his property, beginning with the real estate sign someone has wistfully spray-painted SAVE OUR DESERT. Next comes the gouging and banking, the contouring for artificial lakes and fountains that will depend on shrinking groundwater. Before long the quadrangle is looped with boulevards of townhouses, villas, studio apartments, chalets, ranchettes and palazzos, not to mention such recombinant digs as hometels and lakedominiums, whose very unpronounceability adds a certain grandeur. The names, in fact, have become collectibles. Fountain Hills has a subdevelopment called Clear Aire. In Tempe, near Arizona State University, is a complex called University Shadows, and one imagines a brochure that begins, "As the sun slowly sinks behind the Carl Hayden Library . . ." The well-named Carefree is flush with such thoroughfares as Easy Street, Camelot Circle, and Languid Lane—as if having arrived were synonymous with boredom—and has jockeyed Ho Street and Hum Street so that the sign at the central intersection will read Ho Hum, right where the candle shops flourish. Scottsdale, which annexed 125 square miles in one gulp, may win with a tract that was cleaned of cactus, seeded with haciendas, landscaped with a few fresh cacti from a nursery, and christened Cactus Estates. When such compounds are nearly ready, pyracantha vines with waxy leaves and orange berries are planted around the perimeter to disguise what is no longer a horizon of leopard-spotted mountains, but a wall. Up go the strings of pennants, an American flag is hoisted, a GRAND OPENING! banner is unfurled on the highway, and the desert is open for inspection.

Wright's injunction that civilization abstract the desert's own pattern is nonetheless honored in the eeriest sort of way. Buildings are low, avenues are broad and curving, and the walls are so long that they seem low—making the land still appear open. Streets are named Saguaro Lane, Cholla Place, Ironwood Drive, Jackrabbit Warren and Quail Run, as if honoring the life forms they have replaced. Habitations, sporting names in mangled Spanish, are generally of poured concrete, rounded at the corners, stuccoed to roughen the texture, then sprayed buff, ochre, beige, siennas raw and burnt—the decorator's "Desert Colors"—to simulate adobe. Larger desert plants such as saguaros, agaves, and barrel cacti—bought from nurseries that have, in turn, frequently plundered public lands—are stuck among the more numerous eucalyptus and Russian olive transported from other hemispheres. A development

◆   *103*   ◆

style that was brought to maturity in California has been given the imagery of the Sonoran Desert. This is abstraction of a sort Wright never imagined. It is as if the desert weren't being obliterated so much as geometrized into a Borgesian facsimile, complete with labyrinth. The desert lives—not in the flesh, but as mythology.

Now that the "candy-makers and cactus-hunters" have brought their designer deserts to the brink of Taliesin West, the architectural school that Wright founded in Scottsdale in 1937, the whole notion of a civilization adapted to the desert seems driven to its last corner. Wright, who died in 1959, was spared witnessing what he'd foreseen, nor did he know that the Central Arizona Project would bore its canal straight through his property. But the power lines that also bisect his property are older, and I asked an architecture student whether Wright had lived to see them. "When Mr. Wright heard they were coming," the student replied, "he threatened to burn the place down. He only backed off when he saw that the power people were more inflexible than he was." That would have been typical of Wright, who also threatened to burn his original Taliesin in Spring Green, Wisconsin to spite some tax assessors—after it had already burned twice, tragically, by other means.

But the high command, even at Taliesin West, is no longer so inflexible. On open desert land between the canal and the closest development, Taliesin West has begun a development of its own, called Taliesin Gates. Proceeds from the venture are to help maintain Wright's original buildings and the Frank Lloyd Wright Foundation. The original plan was to create a "total residential environment born of the principle of Organic Architecture" by allowing clients to build only custom plans from Taliesin, to hire Taliesin architects for original plans, or to buy unbuilt plans by Wright himself. Strict control would be exercised over colors, materials, landscaping. Spec houses would be discouraged by requiring builders to sell

Bruce Berger

back to Taliesin rather than to other home owners. When nobody bought, the rules were loosened and land prices cut in half. Builders can now hire any architect they like, spec homes are permitted, and only such infractions as red tile roofs and building materials that are stark white or pitch black are still taboo. When completed, sixty-two homes, eclectic and mostly non-Organic, will occupy seventy-four acres past the usual guard house. Economics may have forced it, but it seems like the final capitulation. The garden Wright found "unequaled in the rest of the world" has been harvested.

The
Telling
Distance

An Architectural Ghost Story

Bruce
Berger

If the forces responsible for the jagged grey ranges around Phoenix had conspired to create, on a dare, some art deco cliff dwellings, they might have come up with the Arizona Biltmore. The façade, long and recessed, is regularly pocked and shadowed as if colonized by cliff swallows, while the interior seems a flow of elegant, rectilinear caves. Formations include cubist villas, annexes, cabañas and a spiked, ten-sided dome, all thrown from the same magma. The tranquility inside and out suggests more of nature than of civilization, particularly the form civilization has taken recently in Phoenix. The Biltmore is well past its fiftieth anniversary, and for a man-made creation to stand a half-century in such dust storms of commerce is itself a feat nearly geological.

Visitors who attended the three-day opening in February, 1929, had no idea they had arrived at an architectural battleground involving America's flamboyant genius, Frank Lloyd Wright. They drove past the gate through a quarter of a mile of open desert, crossed the Arizona Canal, and reached the hotel with its glittering copper roof, reminding them they were in the Copper State. They entered a low foyer divided by a cluster of pillars with staggered shelves for cactus and a ring of small fountains: a desert hanging garden. To one side, under the decagonal dome, lay a cabaret theater of Byzantine geometry. At the end of the foyer the lobby burst upward with what was, and still is, the largest gold leaf ceiling in the world—yet so narrow with its enfolding mezzanine that it kept the human scale.

To the south glistened a Sun Room full of plants; to the north stretched an immense formal dining room. Upstairs lay a complex of rooms and suites, elegantly appointed, no two alike. Grounds included an Olympic-size pool with cabañas, and fourteen villas, each with its own plan. What astounded the eye was that every structure, from the hotel and out-buildings to the bridges over the canal, was constructed of cement blocks with an obsessive angular pattern that harmonized and recombined like the motif of a fugue. The very light fixtures of the lobby were blocks of glass, built into the walls and elaborating the shape. Here was not generic opulence, but monumental sculpture all of a piece—with the massiveness and recurring ornamentation of a Mayan temple.

Even today, when Phoenix development has swept past the Biltmore toward the horizon and vast new resort complexes open yearly, the Biltmore has kept something of a temple's reserve and its mystery. "Don't let anyone tell you Frank Lloyd Wright built it," warn certain locals. "The Biltmore is Wright's unacknowledged masterpiece," affirm others. The fact that until recently the general public could not even enter the grounds unless cleared by the guard house has cast a further veil over the hotel's activities and origins. No Phoenix institution has gathered a richer mythology—or more deserved it.

The Biltmore was daring even before it took shape. In 1927 the McArthurs, a wealthy Chicago family drawn to the desert, began laying plans to develop the center of their 1,200 acres of cactus eight miles east of Phoenix. Albert McArthur, Sr. held the Arizona Dodge franchise. Two of his sons, Warren and Charles, rounded up backing for what was to be a luxury hotel in dude ranch country, and committed the Biltmore hotel chain to running it. It was only natural that the third son, Albert Chase McArthur, Jr., an architect who had studied under Frank Lloyd Wright back at Wright's Oak Park Workshop eighteen years before, should design the buildings. McArthur, all sides concede, is the "architect of record."

Complications began when McArthur chose as his building material the little-known textile block, which Wright had used in a series of experimental houses in Los Angeles in the early twenties. Wright, in *An Autobiography*, claims to have invented it. His son Lloyd, also an architect, disagreed. In a taped conversation with Phoenix architect Brian A. Spencer in Oak Park, Illinois in July, 1974, hitherto unpublished, Lloyd Wright said that in fact *he* invented it to solve the specific problem of holding up someone's balcony in an earthquake zone—but it took the genius of his father to recognize its larger application. Whatever its provenance, the textile block is not the solid object it seems, but consists of a thin square of cement, sometimes impressed with a design in front, and coffered in back for additional lightness. Block is added to block, with steel rods running between and grout holding them tight, weaving a shell of great textile strength. Walls consist of parallel shells—one facing out, one facing in—with a hollow in between to retain heat in winter and cool in summer. Textured blocks can be placed in various configurations, altered with plain ones or blocks of different patterns, so that the wall forms an abstract tapestry integral with the structure itself. They were still cement blocks, said Wright, but educated.

Even Wright had never used the textile block for anything grander than a few private homes, and here was Albert Chase McArthur, Jr.—with few buildings to his credit—planning to use textile blocks to raise a two-hundred-room, four-story luxury hotel. Recognizing he was beyond his depth, McArthur offered his old mentor $10,000 to come out and help. Since Wright's break with his own master, Louis Sullivan, in 1893, it was hardly his nature to work under anybody else—particularly a former student. In 1927, however, Wright was deeply in debt, hounded by reporters because of personal scandals,

Bruce
Berger

offered few commissions, and facing a particularly nasty winter at Taliesin, his architectural school in Spring Green, Wisconsin. He had been friends with the McArthur family back in Chicago, and had built a house for the parents in the 1890s. Here was a chance to make money, elude the press, and escape to the sun in good company; perhaps in solving Albert's problems he could solve his own.

Wright never traveled lightly. He reached Phoenix by train with his third wife Olgivanna and two small children, and installed them in one of several homes owned by the McArthurs and built by Albert. Wright was thunderstruck by the Arizona desert, revealed to him for the first time, and which he described as a "vast battleground of Titanic natural forces." Its great spaces, its intricate cactus, its low-lying mountains were to become inspirations for many later works, and ten years later he established Taliesin West, a winter home for his architectural school, the Frank Lloyd Wright Foundation, some twenty miles northeast of the Biltmore. With typical demonism he set to work on the McArthurs' hotel, lingering through summer when temperatures reached 118 degrees.

Although Wright was an instinctive rather than a trained engineer, he easily supervised the casting of a quarter of a million textile blocks from desert sand right on the property. But Wright, in his cape and broad-brimmed hat, brandishing his cane, fifty-seven years old and world-renowned, could hardly be expected to remain the humble engineer and draftsman for an old apprentice. An employee of Wright's named George Kastner visited the Biltmore construction site, and reported the charged atmosphere in a letter to a friend in Milwaukee. His two-car party was stopped at the gate by men with sticks, who denied them entrance because they didn't have a pass. Kastner talked the guards into letting him in alone to look for McArthur. A few workers had seen McArthur within the hour, but most didn't know him at all. Kastner finally got his party past the goons with a doctored pass from a stranger he met on the site. Wright showed up with his family and gave Kastner the grand tour. Kastner pointed out a light that was not encased in a glass block, and Wright, obsessed by the omission, kept snapping, "Rotten!" Wright then led the crew on a wild motor chase through the desert after dark because he wanted to check out some back roads on the way home. Kastner left little doubt which architect he found in charge.

It seems clear that any fondness Wright and McArthur may have had for each other was dispelled by their collaboration. Lloyd Wright, in the taped interview, describes Albert McArthur as a professional student, a twenty-year Ivy Leaguer who never got up before eleven, and who never forgave Wright for getting unofficial credit for a building that only Wright, after all, could have built. The elder Wright was hardly less scathing, and complained in his autobiography that Albert was a "rich man's son" who couldn't control his engineers. Wright strongly objected to the fourth floor, which would have been unnecessary if they had only built more cottages. Worse, the contractors apparently didn't trust the strength of the textile blocks and filled the hollows between them with traditional cement, adding hundreds of thousands of dollars to the cost and turning the blocks into mere decoration. To the observer, of course, the cement between the blocks is invisible and irrelevant, but Wright could clearly see through walls to a violation of principle, and felt insulted. As for the added expense, Wright remarks that money was of no consequence to the builders, and he had no authority over the matter besides "bullying Albert." He concludes the passage in *An Autobiography* by remarking that Albert ought to tell the story of the Biltmore as a warning to young architects, but was probably "too near it yet, too personally involved in its various equivocal implications, *meum* and *tuum*, to tell it straight, even to himself probably, for another twenty years." Unburdened of this sarcasm, Wright declines to tell the

Bruce
Berger

story himself, presumably because it would be unethical to attack the "architect of record."

The McArthur family, however, has not been amused by the notion that their Albert was not chiefly responsible for a masterpiece with his name on it. Charles McArthur, Albert's brother and one of the hotel's backers, wrote to *Arizona Highways* in 1956 to say that Albert deliberately designed it in the "spirit" of Frank Lloyd Wright, and that he paid Wright $10,000 for the right to use the textile block and for technical information on how it worked— and that was to be the limit of Wright's involvement. It was a shock, he said, when Wright showed up with family in tow, moved in, and interfered with every phase of the project until he had to be asked to leave. Wright's widow Olgivanna, on the other hand, recalls that Wright was summoned to Arizona by telegram by Albert, and Bruce Pfeiffer, archivist at Taliesin West, has said that the McArthur family turned over the Wright-McArthur correspondence to the Frank Lloyd Wright Foundation upon Wright's death, with the stipulation that it never be made public. Through the crossfire one glimpses two men caught in an impossible situation: Albert, out of his depth as an architect but with a prestigious family name to uphold, and Wright, a spontaneous genius forced to take orders from a student who couldn't control his underlings. Olgivanna Wright has said that her husband "was never famous as a man who willingly made any compromises," and many also felt that Wright was not above starting a few human brush fires for his own amusement.

In the wake of such human frailty, it is perhaps the buildings themselves that should speak. It is generally held that the configuration of the large spaces and the design on the textile block were McArthur's. But the proportions of the lobby, its surrounding mezzanine, the way its inset lights continue the building's motif, are too like the lobby of Wright's previous Imperial Hotel in Tokyo to be coincidental, while the Aztec Room, under its multi-faceted dome, echoes the Imperial's Peacock Room. As for the Mayan look, Wright was an admirer of pre-Columbian forms, and mirrored them in his earlier textile block buildings in Los Angeles. David Henry, a forty-seven-year-old Phoenician who began studying Wright's work at the age of eleven, has looked into Albert McArthur's other work to see if any of it resembled the Biltmore. "There was nothing I could find," he said, "that could touch the Biltmore for sheer virtuosity or mastery of space." If the buildings are to speak, they suggest that in 1927 Albert McArthur was roundly bullied by the master.

Those who attended the grand opening were less interested in such architectural *meum* and *tuum* than they were in lobster thermidor, boned squab, and dancers from Spain, South America and the Hopi Reservation. Prohibition was circumvented by a men's lounge up a back stairway, featuring a full bar and a fireplace with perforated textile blocks so tipplers could watch sparks weave up the chimney; ladies and mixed couples had drinks slipped to them more discreetly on the terrace. But February 1929 was only months before the stock market crash, and by the end of the year the McArthur family had sold the Biltmore and surrounding properties to William Wrigley, Jr., the chewing gum mogul—another Chicago millionaire and a friend of the family. The swimming pool had been lined with tile from Catalina Island, which the Wrigleys happened to own, and they had no trouble maintaining standards.

The Biltmore, catering to those with their money intact, sailed through the Depression and the War. The main building housed a billiard room, stock market board, barber shop, soda fountain and branches of exclusive Phoenix shops, while the grounds offered lawn bowling, a small racetrack for horses, skeet shooting range, picnic area, and a stable with trails winding into pure desert. One

Bruce Berger

employee tended a covey of domestic quail so that diners could be assured of fresh quail eggs. If the Biltmore was considered a trifle stuffy by the denizens of Phoenix's raucous downtown, it drew a national clientele of millionaires, politicians, movie stars and celebrities—not excluding Frank Lloyd Wright, who motored with his entourage from Taliesin West to dine in the center of the Gold Room. He still publicly denied credit for the Biltmore, no doubt enjoying whispers at surrounding tables that he was, nonetheless, responsible for it all.

The Wrigleys maintained the resort with little change for forty-four years, escaping Chicago winters to supervise operations from their Spanish-style mansion on a nearby hill. At last too old to travel, they sold the Biltmore in 1973 to Talley Industries, a holding company based in Mesa, Arizona. Talley promised to maintain the traditional style, but many Phoenicians wondered whether a corporation could show a personal commitment.

The Telling Distance

What Phoenix saw on June 20, three weeks after the sale was consummated, was smoke billowing from the hotel's top story as engines raced to the city's first six-alarm fire. If one believed that ghosts return to haunt the places that vexed them, one might suspect Wright, fourteen years deceased, had returned to destroy the fourth floor he so abominated. The inspector's explanation is that a spark from a welder's torch ignited some insulation material in the top crawl space. The hotel was closed for the summer, sparing death or injury, but the entire top floor was destroyed and much of the copper roof had caved in. Smoke from the fire and water from the fire department had so ravaged the furniture, carpets and drapes that every furnishing in the building had to be pitched out.

Talley Industries, put to the test more summarily than expected, had planned to reopen on September 29, had booked a convention on opening day, and was determined to keep its commitment. They consulted several architectural firms, then hired the obvious choice: the Frank Lloyd

Wright Foundation. The Foundation usually packed up every June to work until November in the cool of Taliesin East, but in 1973 the entire outfit, student-apprentices and faculty, camped in the heat of the Biltmore and worked around the clock.

The Biltmore's original décor, for all its splendor, had been eclectic, with designs by McArthur, designs by Wright, designs by unknowns. But the archives of the Foundation were full of Wright's plans for tables, chairs, panels and lamps, many of which had never been used. Also in the mid-twenties Wright had designed a year's worth of covers for *Liberty Magazine*, an abstract theme for each issue, considered too forward at the time and never run, but full of useful motifs for carpets, curtains and menus. There was grille work from 1908, octagonal tables from 1932, chairs and sofas from the fifties, carpet designs from all stages of his career. What the architects proposed was to replace the random décor with nothing less than a Frank Lloyd Wright museum.

Many of the techniques for making such appointments were lost, and the crew had exactly eighty-eight days. The rugs, using Wright's patterns of triangles, arcs and squares, were custom-woven in Ireland. No one knew how to apply gold leaf, so the men who did the original job in 1928 were brought out of retirement and taught fifteen architects the technique. The new copper of the fourth floor roof didn't match the forty-four-year patina of what survived, so Talley Industries developed a new chemical aging formula. Fresh textile blocks were made on the site from molds that had been saved. Blocks that withstood the blaze had to be steamed and resteamed to pry out the stench of smoke. One of the architectural students was noted for his keen nose, and after each scouring they sent him through the lobby and said, "Dennis, tell us if it's *still* there."

The centerpiece of the designs provided by the Foundation was a panel of saguaro cactus forms Wright created

Bruce Berger

with compass, triangle and T-square while he worked on the Biltmore. Cactus had seized his imagination. He studied their inner workings, found in the ribbed construction of the saguaro a natural analogue to his steel-ribbed textile blocks, and in the cellular barrel cactus a parallel to the way his walls grew block upon block. Like a desert messiah, he felt he had created an architecture for man that would "qualify him in a human habitation to become a godlike native part of Arizona." By creating saguaro forms with compass and T-square he was artistically completing the circle, turning architecture back into cactus. He tried many versions, never satisfied, and the Foundation commissioned one of them to be reproduced by Nino Grieco of Tempe, Arizona, in acrylic plastic. It had to be hauled to the Biltmore by open truck, and so fearful were they that it would prove a tempting target for rock-throwing kids that it was transported in the hours before dawn, September 29. On opening morning it was empaneled next to the hanging garden in the foyer, illumined from behind, and greeted conventioneers and the public to a fresh, sweet-smelling Biltmore more permeated with Wright than ever. If Wright witched the fire, it paid off.

Wright believed in an architecture that would permit growth, and the Biltmore grew. Under the Wrigleys, Talley Industries, and more recently a Canadian group, a grand ballroom, a conference center and several new guest buildings were added, bringing the room total to more than five hundred. All of the additions have been designed by architects from the Frank Lloyd Wright Foundation, and all appear to have been made of textile blocks. Real textile blocks are now too labor-intensive and costly to manufacture, and these are decorative panels thrown in front of traditional concrete. If Wright still sees through walls he is probably seeing red, but the new buildings probably merit the best that can be said for additions to a masterpiece—they are stashed to the side and in back, and expand the facilities economically while, esthetically, they fail to offend.

The moods of affluence have forced other changes. Gone are the billiard room, the market board, the barber shop, the soda fountain, the skeet range, the stable; installed are the tennis courts, the exercise salon, the jacuzzi, the second golf course. With Prohibition a forgotten joke, the Aztec Room has become a cocktail lounge with dancing, while the secret men's lounge is now the office for the catering service. A most successful transformation is conversion of the Sun Room into the Orangerie, a restaurant with beaded lights cast into stalactite chandeliers, some of the most elaborate food in the Valley—and a menu with an old *Liberty Magazine* motif. A pleasing anachronism is the chess set with three-foot knights and bishops for stand-up matches by the pool. More symptomatic is the mammoth convention center for people who come to places like the Biltmore to confuse business with pleasure.

Bruce
Berger

If the Biltmore has absorbed expansion and the advent of Lifestyles with composure, the same cannot be said for the surrounding desert. As the flash flood of humanity swept the valley to make Phoenix the largest city between Dallas and Los Angeles, Phoenicians were grateful for that 1,200 acres of mostly open cactus, and considered it sacrosanct. They were alarmed when Biltmore Fashion Park bit off one corner in the late sixties: elegant, but still a shopping center. In 1973 the Frank Lloyd Wright Foundation master-planned the entire area, and Talley began letting contracts to private developers. Gone with the riding and skeet shooting was the famous Pink Sidewalk that meandered to the hotel's private reservoir, useful not only to guests but to young locals who snuck in for courtship rites. Gone is most of the cactus that Wright and the McArthurs so loved. Now open to the public is a townhouse complex called Biltmore Gates. Also Biltmore

Greens, Biltmore Colony, Biltmore Courts, Biltmore Circle, Biltmore Square, The Heights of Biltmore, plus a few private homes and corporate headquarters. Wright found Los Angeles in the twenties to be full of ersatz Spanish missions, and here are their crabbed descendents: replicated villas with blinding white walls, pitched roofs of orange and blue tile, arched entryways and Mediterranean trim, cramped in mazes of curving drives—all that Wright called *realtoresque*. The lover of the Biltmore can only rejoice that the developments are screened by walls of stucco and oleander, distanced by fairways, and perhaps deaden the roar of Phoenix even better than well-spaced saguaros. If Wright designed an architecture to fit man for the desert, here is the proof no one noticed.

If it seems that the master has overwhelmed the forgotten McArthur, it is worth remembering that architecture is more an art of collaboration, like a movie, than a single inspiration, like a poem. Leading architects, like Renaissance painters, have apprentices, draftsmen and associates who flesh out an original conception, which is then at the mercy of clients and contractors. Architects steal from each other on a ritual basis, and new ideas become public spoils. McArthur was Wright's student before he was his boss, and Wright wasn't above lifting from his own son. Now that fifty years have passed, only heirs speak for the protagonists, and numerous architects have had a hand in the Biltmore's latter career. Perhaps we should see the Biltmore as a great collaboration, a synthesis of what desert architecture could be. It is early to tell, but after the free-wheeling plague of townhouses, ranchettes and jerrybuilt villas has crumbled back to the far sands, as crumble they must, the Biltmore may remain with the hills it resembles, peacefully watching.

PINIONS, PIÑONS,

AND OPINIONS

Birdwatching: An Initiation

D espite the example of Audubon, who shot thousands of the birds he so lovingly committed to paint, bird-watching has had an air of ethereality, of soft-heartedness, of passivity a little suspect in our democracy on the make. I knew this even in the sixth grade, when I ordered a bird caller from a novelty catalogue. That was the year birds leapt into view, and I opened the small brown package a little breathlessly. Inside was a clever metallic plug attached to a thumb ring and fitting in a red wooden peg, so that when the metal was twisted in the wood it chittered vaguely like a finch. I rushed outside and tried it. Nothing flew to my side, nor did the cry sound like anything in suburban Chicago, but I would be patient and explore the neighborhood.

As soon as I left our property I felt like a fugitive. What would I say if an adult or larger child asked me what I was doing with field glasses and a bird caller when all the other young men were at football scrimmage? I slunk through the alleys, hid behind lilacs and twisted the thumb ring. If I was heard and not seen I would be taken for a bird. When I thought of encountering humanity my cheeks burned and my heart pounded. If I wanted to chase birds, I thought logically, whose business was it? I would act as if it were perfectly average. But I knew it wasn't. A little boy birdwatcher would be jeered at, perhaps beaten up, and I wanted desperately to be like everyone else.

Much as I loved my red and silver bird caller, the birds

didn't, and when my slinks were all potential embarrassment and no birds, I kept my hobby at home. I made a small wooden feeder in manual training, suspended it outside my window, and stocked it with the pet shop mix. Next to it I hung a board with wires to impale a severed orange, and inside the room I positioned a camera with a cable so that I could stand just out of sight, behind a floor lamp, and snap whatever came. The oriole and grosbeak shots were impressive. But the local diversity—cardinals, grosbeaks, orioles, blue jays, and scores of clamorous little sparrows—was soon exhausted, and months passed without novelty. Worst of all, the blue jays would swoop in screeching at first light, prop sunflower seeds edgewise between their claws and jackhammer them open before even I, always first up, was awake. My passion for birds lasted a year.

Bruce Berger

Free of adolescence and suburbia, I felt secure—even powerful—with bird book and binoculars. The emergence of the environmental movement had elevated bird-watching to a metaphor for sentimental interference with the goose-step of progress. Birdwatchers were those bleeders who could magically stop highways, de-authorize dams and fell power plants with a smart remark at a hearing, or a note to a congressman. Yet through high school, college, and years of post-graduate drifting, I recall only the vaguest interest in actual birds. I was proud to be a birdwatcher by repute, but I seldom looked up.

It wasn't until I had a house of my own that I dutifully bought a *Peterson's Guide* and hung up a feeder. But a more serious birder next door put out a spread that included tins of peanut butter and suet in wire cages, inheriting strays hundreds of miles off course, while my Audubon seed tube drew the usual leftover sparrows. After the death of my German shepherd, stray cats invaded the yard, hid in the shrubbery, waited for birds to clean up the seeds that fell to the ground, then struck. Dogs, I realized, were unwitting protectors of birds. Since there was no way to persuade a condominium full of cat lovers to restrain or bell their beloved killers, and since my dogless feeder had become a death trap, I gave up.

But that adult year of feeding sparrows reactivated my childhood fever. Birds took roost in my psyche. Those descendants of flying lizards, those twists of the spectrum, those mobilized jewels, represented the most ferocious visible compaction of sheer life. The mere fact of them was stunning. I bought other bird books, more powerful binoculars. Walking or driving, my eye followed everything in flight. A mere awareness of birds infused a day with microscopic adventures. Driving through open country and spotting a raptor, I would slam the brakes, pull over and grab the glasses, and have considered ordering a bumper sticker that says, I STOP FOR HAWKS. Journal entries, increasingly, were of birds. A few:

September 23, 1978

Drilling Chopin at the upright piano, which walls off sight of all but itself, I became aware of an accompaniment like sleighbells. The mountain ash outside the window, sagging with orange berries, had burst into frantic, ravenous birds, half of them pale green, the other half pink above and brown below. Emissaries from the sun? The bird book showed them to be pine grosbeaks, transients I was unaware of.

October 3, 1978

Birds seem so exempt from gravity, so composed of air itself, that there is a perverse appeal to any species that shows its bulk. Whenever a magpie lands on the scrub oak outside my window, the usual domain of warblers and sparrows, something in my own bulk responds. At first the magpie seems too big for reality, like a 747 in a flock of Cessnas. As if doing a warbler impression, the huge bird moves nimbly through the leaves, occasional bits of green flashing from his mouth. And every time he changes perch, giving a little boost with both feet and a half-flap of the wings, the branch he lights on is set thrashing up and down, its whole sector of leaves in an uproar. In the course of ravenous feeding, advancing in jerks and darts, plotting his way with hard shiny eyes, the magpie finally animates the whole tree. Gravity may be democratic, tugging evenly on us all, but it is the bulky bird, seeming too large for the vegetable world that trembles beneath it, that makes you feel in your bones the wistfulness of flight.

October 16, 1978

Bruce Berger

We prepared to camp on a high plateau in Utah, a land almost clean of birds, when a complicated call floated from some far piñons. I grabbed the binoculars and began stalking. There was something about the pattern, a kind of double loop that returned to the same note, that reminded me of the symbol for infinity, or perhaps a Moebius strip. As the call got louder and still eluded me, I became more excited. At last I spotted the source on a piñon top and trained the glasses, to my horror, on an American robin. Here was a bird that had surrounded me all my life, and it took this remote forest to make me listen.

December 3, 1978

I stopped at the Bosque del Apache Wildlife Refuge south of Albuquerque. Hundreds of sandhill cranes, grey and lean, stood in open fields near the Rio Grande. Their mass emitted a loud hollow rumbling, and waves of movement seemed continually to pass through them, causing a few at a time to stretch their wings and hop a foot or two, as if ruffled by a common internal breeze. One whooping crane stood among them, taller and pure white, a prima ballerina. Later I followed a trail through the high grass, one of the few places one is allowed on foot. A flock of sandhill cranes flew overhead in streamlined, arrowlike shapes, and suddenly the grass around crepitated as if with a soft rain or a hail of pellets. It was a moment before I realized that what I was hearing, and fortunately not feeling, was a shower of crane droppings.

December 27, 1978

I spent the day exploring the Provincial Museum in Victoria, B. C., and came upon cases of stuffed birds representing half the species in North America. Here was a chance to bone up on details of marking even better than I could with the best photos and drawings. After fifteen minutes I became depressed—not because my brain grew stale or the specimens were dead, but because the birds looked so much smaller than they do in life. Does the process of taxidermy actually shrink them, or does the animation of life make them look larger than they really are?

November 7, 1979

Walking out the drive to get the morning paper at my mother's house outside Phoenix, I noticed the top hole in a saguaro cactus was plugged with an ill-defined mass of grey like a rat's nest. When I approached the grey withdrew, leaving the hole black. Somewhere inside was grey matter, alive.

November 8, 1979

I snuck out early with binoculars, hid behind a palo verde, and the rat's nest resolved into a small face with its eyes closed as if sunning itself: an owl. My guide books were unhelpful, but a volume at the library stated that only two species of owl roost in the saguaro, and since the elf owl was too small, the face belonged to a screech owl. Surrounded by green pulp, it reminded me oddly of an almond stuffed in an olive.

February 2, 1980

Just north of Fort Huachuca on a morning blank with fog, I pulled off to peer through a rift to a ridge dazzling with sable rocks and snow. In the foreground stood a piñon filled with red-winged blackbirds making a racket like gurgling windchimes, with one silent hawk on top. It was like a Christmas tree with blackbirds for ornaments and a hawk for a star. Given a massive choice of trees, why were both species on the same one? I later asked two experienced birders, one of whom replied that blackbirds and hawks are not necessarily enemies, and the other that perhaps the blackbirds were keeping an eye on the hawk. One wonders about experts . . .

February 19, 1980

I lay on my back in a wash below Four Peaks, watching a red-tail through the field glasses, when it dropped a heroic strand of white like three feet of clothesline.

April 17, 1980

Who could be flying a kite, and at such an altitude, where only a jeep track wound through miles of volcanic tuff? I grabbed the glasses, and the long-tailed shape soaring upward resolved into a hawk with a lengthy snake in its talons. I had to laugh at the implicit pun, for a kite is one of the groups of the hawk family. This was God's kite . . .

May 24, 1980

Seldom has the sheer poignancy of a bird so struck me: the red plush on the cap and throat, the custard under-feathers, the intricately peppered wings, back and tail. I had marveled at the same species once in my yard; now here it was in a sandstone canyon quietly tapping holes in a tree, waiting for the sap to ooze out, feeding on the trapped insects. Sympathy with other creatures comes unbidden, and I felt a sudden connection with this

Bruce
Berger

obscure life, so physically vibrant, so committed to its odd destiny from tree to tree. I also knew my trance was beginning to pall on a companion unused to long stares at mute phenomena. Perhaps the very sense of my friend's discomfort—not wanting to disturb me but bored beyond endurance—further honed my perception. But I knew my time with this creature was limited, and how it would end.

"What kind of bird is it?" whispered my friend.

I considered lying. "A yellow-bellied sapsucker."

"You have to be kidding. There actually *is* a yellow-bellied sapsucker?"

I clung to the bird. "You're looking at it."

"Be serious. Jack Benny made that up."

"No," I said, watching the creature turn to mirage even as it quietly tapped the bark. "It's a real bird." I fixed on the deep red feathers, the even rows of holes, the progress from tree to tree. Sweet life without words.

"A yellow-bellied sapsucker," repeated my friend as if filing an anecdote. "Ten minutes in front of a yellow-bellied sapsucker."

June 16, 1980

A friend phoned me that sapsuckers were nesting in an eye-level hole in one of his dead aspens, in case I wanted to come over. We watched from a distance as the mother flew out of an opening that seemed half her diameter, glided back a few minutes later to muffled shrieks, squeezed inside to feed her brood, then flew off again. After one of her exits we crept to the hole. There was no peering into the darkness, but we took turns listening. The birds apparently thought it was a food-bearing mother rather than a human ear that darkened their world, and let loose with a screeching only inches from the tympanum that left my right ear ringing as if it had just been through a disco.

October 2, 1980

A magazine usually devoted to heroic backpacks,

desperate river runs and ascents of north faces ran an orange and scarlet telephoto cover of some geese crossing the sun. A feature article on birdwatching: perhaps contemplation had come of age. The story, it turned out, concerned a young man who had tried to break the record for the number of species sighted in North America during one calendar year, and spent increasing sums jetting to ever remoter locales as time ran out. No suspicious lingering to admire feathers, none of the wonder of birds at all beyond the cover photo—the feature proved that birdwatching could engage one's manhood as thoroughly as kayaking Lava Falls or getting frostbite on Denali. The credit card birder may have had facets not covered by the article, but the author was clearly one of the kids from football scrimmage.

Bruce
Berger

September 23, 1981

Below windshield level was a flash of grey that refused to deflect, and that reappeared as a limp pile in the rearview mirror. Alone on a gravel road in eastern Oregon, I backed up to see what I'd hit. The bird was unbelievably soft, the skull a tough little acorn on a loose, boneless neck. There was a clean, art deco quality to the charcoal grey back, the grey head with black mask, the black wings that pulled out to reveal pure white medallions, the fierce hooked beak. It was a loggerhead shrike. I remembered an old movie called *The Shrike,* based on the myth that the female kills the male after mating, and starring a menacingly saccharine June Allyson. But the bird in my hand seemed genderless, I was the hapless killer, and the shrike seemed an unmythical creature making its way in earnest.

October 6, 1981

Recently I watched a cowbird going berserk along a mirrored window, raising one wing and then the other, feinting, jabbing the glass, hovering a foot away to gather force for the next attack, driving off the rival cowbird that was himself. And this afternoon I traced an odd scratching to a sill where a fly batted itself against the bottom of a clear window and a female Wilson's warbler hopped outside in tandem, trying to stab the fly through the glass. Birds that hurl themselves against windows they take for continuing blue sky and are killed, or momentarily stunned, have little time to ponder the deception. But what of the cowbird and the warbler? We assume that birds live wholly in the present and fly off with their instinct intact, neither suffering psychoses nor reporting religious experiences. But for us their minds are necessarily off-limits, and to imagine shifts in their worldview only throws us back on ourselves with our mirages, our tricks like glass that pit the senses against each other, saying yes to the eyes and no to the beak, and causing the insect wings to beat against the impenetrable light until they expire.

November 28, 1982

It strikes me that in humanity I appreciate a quiet, withdrawn, non-combative quality once praised as gentleness and now put down as wimpiness, while in birds I am drawn to raptors, predators and scavengers—the crows and hawks, falcons and shrikes—birds that swoop upon other birds or the recent dead. Is some suppressed viciousness surfacing in birdwatching? Is it vicarious liberation from moral choice? Whatever the motive, what revenge to discover the magpie jay, a bird with the brattiest qualities of both its namesakes and a rakish crest all its own. In gangs they terrorize the Oaxacan roadsides, flitting arrogantly from tree to tree, bouncing the branches, their eyes running with mascara, screeching, brawling, refusing to follow the lead's command. What splendid arrogance! What relief they're not people.

December 2, 1982

A love of birds resembles, visually, a love for flowers, as well as a taste for creations in precious metals and gems. A case in point is the russet-crowned motmot, a foot-long bird we spotted by the Chiapan roadside, in silhouette as if poised for display. The eye is a dark ruby with a black center, set in a streak of lapis and shadowed by malachite; the beak is hooked onyx; the crown is of amber; and the slender body, with undersides of pale citron, tapers to twin black tail feathers whose webbing is plucked near the tips so that the points hang like pendants. Peterson's *Field Guide to Mexican Birds* shows the russet-crowned motmot as the drabbest bird on the page, but the sight of it in person makes even Yeats' bird of "hammered gold and gold enameling" seem a comparative sparrow.

May 9, 1983

Over the years I have identified such false birds as dead leaves, mesquite beans, pine cones, seed pods, insulators and chipmunks. And this morning on the San Juan River I saw the flash of a snowy egret that turned out to be a kayak paddle.

November 4, 1983

How strange that a hummingbird should return to the nest outside the window in November, months ahead of schedule. And such an odd hummingbird—instead of sitting beady-eyed midair in a variety of poses before lighting, it sped to and fro like a relay runner. I picked up the glasses from across the room: the bird was a black-tailed gnatcatcher recycling the hummingbird nest for its own new home.

November 23, 1984

Nothing suggestive of music is so hard to hear with precision as the calls of birds. High-pitched, irregular in rhythm, fluent in semi-tones, birds can baffle the ear still more than they frustrate the eye, and even an opera buff may have difficulty with the leitmotifs of lapwings and warblers. How surprising, then, to come across the music

Bruce Berger

of Olivier Messiaen, in which birds in all their elusiveness come to life on that well-tempered machine, the piano.

Messiaen generally tells you on the score or in the record notes when he is trying to suggest a particular species, but even where he doesn't one senses that a specific bird is behind the passage. There is surely no point, musically, to literal ornithology, and even if there were, these are times when composers don't hesitate to write duets for piano and tape, and an actual bittern could be spliced in as needed. What Messiaen manages is the likeness of birds in a musical context, a repertoire of effects that seems eerie but in place. He adds, at times, an extra-musical intent, as in the fifth section of *Vingt Regards sur L'Enfant-Jésus,* when the presumed joy of birds at the birth of Christ is evoked with grace notes and rapid polytonal figurations in the upper register, over mid-register chords that Messiaen has identified as the theme of God. You would have to be told that the lower chords were playing God, but there is no mistaking the strato-sphere of birds going about the upheaval of being birds while ignoring whatever non-threatening activity is going on below them.

Composers from Vivaldi to Beethoven to Granados to Stravinsky have worked bird effects into their scores—the typical upshot of which is the generic spring celebrant, the two-note cuckoo, or that romantic quack, the nightingale. To create pieces of varying textures around a whole catalogue of species, on an instrument that cannot repro-duce their intervals—and make music—suggests that Messiaen may have listened to birds themselves more closely than his predecessors. In turning literal cries into art, Messiaen has illuminated, perhaps inadvertently, a paradox about birds, and even about art itself. With a biologically limited range of sound, consisting of little more than the same phrase over and over, birds seem utterly programmed—and at the same time wholly spon-taneous. So it can happen in art, that a set of arbitrary constraints has been so internalized, so dominated, that the barriers disappear and the voice breaks free.

January 23, 1985

I was walking an arroyo at dusk outside Florence, Arizona, when from the gathering dark and silence came a high-pitched squalling from a single dense hackberry bush. As I approached, a stream of panicked bushtits went off like fireworks around me, while with heart-stopping booms a covey of quail burst from the leafy depths. I made my way slowly around the bush, every few steps setting off new charges of bushtits and quail, a whole powder magazine of confetti and grenades, until I had recklessly emptied the whole bush. I returned earlier next evening for a more studied look at this cohabitation of species, but there was not a bird to be seen; in my excitement I had apparently ruined the neighborhood.

Bruce Berger

February 16, 1985

Shot up with Demerol in the wake of an operation for a burst appendix, I had a vision of a multi-flowered hummingbird feeder zinging with hummingbirds, and one tiny helicopter, refueling.

March 17, 1986

The staghorn cholla supports three cactus wren nests at staggered levels, each some three feet from the others. It is a cactus wren trick to build several fake nests near the real one, so that the mother can lead a predator to the wrong nest and guard it with mock ferocity. Homes and false fronts are equally slack assemblies of twigs, dried leaves, bits of string—anything that can be unlittered from the desert floor—so situated that cactus joints rather than sound engineering hold them together. What distinguishes this particular suite is that the wren has managed to weave several yards of white toilet paper through each nest and loop it unbroken between them, much as the gauze in a painting of the Three Graces artfully links the figures while preserving their chastity. Whether a predator could follow this paper chase to the baby wrens is a matter the Darwinian forces haven't had much time to work on.

March 4, 1987

A Heermann's Gull flew over the lagoon at the mouth of the Carmel River with a large yellow object in its bill. It lit at the water's edge, near where I was sitting. Binoculars blew up the object to half a petrified Twinkie, too huge to swallow. The bird shook it in its coral beak, then dropped it in the sand. It took it up again, shook it with lowered head so that sand flew in both directions, put it back down and pecked at loosened crumbs. It repeated this maneuver several times and the tough dough, still oversized, visibly shrank. The gull stabbed and chipped more off. When the yellow was down to half its original size, the bird made a reckless gulp, and like a snake committed to a rodent, started the quarter-Twinkie down its throat. With a bit of dancing the meal was down. The bird made a few more pecks for crumbs, then sipped some brackish water for a chaser. It stood for a minute looking blank as an account-ant, then, chore completed, flapped off.

October 2, 1987

An ear for birdsong can become so obsessive that during daylight hours the birder refuses to play records or turn on the radio, always remotely sifting the racket outside for an unfamiliar species to stalk and identify. But what was this high single note that refused to repeat for an entire day, or for so many days that one forgot about it? How could one pursue a bird that only called once? Yet that sharp cry was as loud as a mockingbird, so loud it almost seemed inside the house. And didn't I hear it once in the middle of the night? At last it sounded straight over my head and I identified it as the distress call of the smoke alarm, lamenting its dying battery.

January 21, 1988

Was hiking a canyon out of Mexia when a red-tailed hawk burst from the shrubbery practically at my feet and lit on the nearest *cardón*. As I pinned him in the binoculars, something from his feet rose like a trick rope and opened enormous jaws: a snake. The hawk jabbed at the gaping mouth, caught hold, pulled, and the snake, amazingly, appeared to stretch like elastic. As the hawk ripped off pieces and swallowed, filaments of the snake thinned like strands of mozzarella. The tearing, yanking and swallowing continued for some two minutes until the hawk slurped up the tail as if drawing in a last strand of spaghetti. He poked a bit at his feet, cleaning his talons, then sat perfectly still. A sudden tremor passed all the way through him, ruffling his feathers, perhaps shaking down the meal. The hawk gazed serenely a few minutes more, then glided off.

*Bruce
Berger*

February 29, 1988

I celebrated Leap Year Day by walking out on the Death Valley saltpan. Though the sun bore down and kiln-glazed escarpments towered above me, the valley floor of salt, soft underfoot and glistening for miles, inevitably reminded me of snow. When I raised my binoculars to decipher a black speck in the distance, I involuntarily pictured a brown-capped rosy finch—a bird I looked for in tundra snowfields last July. Another quarter of a mile brought me to the speck itself, indeed a bird.

Alone with its blue shadow, it was a dead crow. Its feet were folded into its belly; otherwise it was intact. What feathers you could see were in disarray, stripped of their iridescence and bleached to an ash, but most of the bird was crusted with glittering crystals of salt. The eye sockets shone with a pure white concentration, as if to meet the sun's own stare, and only the bill protruded with its impermeable horn. Saline moisture had apparently filtered upward from the saltpan by capillary action, which draws water solutions through anything porous. Heat and drought had burned off the water, leaving salt to crystallize on the feathers like hoarfrost. I was reminded of the elaborate crystal salt dishes used at Versailles, here imitated by an actual bird that fell by chance, to begin its lone transmigration into the mineral kingdom.

Most journals betray a greater leaning toward prejudice and romance than scientific rigor, and this one slights the birdwatcher for the bird. As a latecomer to birding and non-member of the Audubon Society I have doubtless missed the full range of birdwatchers, but suspect their diversity approximates that of birds. And I have identified the dreary little squabblers. These are the rabid taxonomists, the detail jocks who know—as if birds were cars—all the eye rings, the wing bars, the curvature of beaks, the lengths of tail. Off they go, pad in hand, after the new find. But their thrill is not rarity as such but the addition of one more sighting. Scaled-down versions of the sprinter in the magazine article, they are vying to see how many species they can spot in a given gulch, or on a single Memorial Day, and the birder with the highest body count wins. At their most ludicrous they keep what is known as a "life list," a count of the species they have identified between birth and death. I look forward to the first tomb inscribed, "He Saw 1,067 Species of Birds Before He Croaked." As technicians they are virtuosos. They can distinguish between the multitudes of sparrows they resemble and which impressively swell their count, and by scoring the species everyone else misses they make one realize how blind (or else how honest) the rest of us are. The wonder of birds must have struck them when they began, or they'd have found something else to quantify, but somewhere along the line—through boredom, lack of imagination, or the ritual of groups—they lost the way. And it is they who have corrupted the joy, for the number-buffs have introduced what birdwatching as romance so gloriously lacks:

competition. Their champion's favorite bird is his boring self.

At the opposite pole is the professional ornithologist. The bird lister's goal, identification, is his starting point. Using mist nets, banding, photography, computers, volumes of data and a lifetime of patience, his mission is to understand the bird. He must determine its food, its territory, its life cycle, the fluctuations of the species, its niche in the biosphere—even, perhaps, its well-being as an indicator of an area's environmental health. But the ornithologist too runs his risk. If he is to know birds thoroughly, birdwatching for him cannot be a mere diversion among many, and given the range even of birds he will have to specialize. It will finally be plovers or pigeons, hawks or hummingbirds. And no matter what bird he chooses, and how much he finds out, the bird will escape in the end.

Bruce Berger

Where does that leave the oaf who simply likes to look at birds? Teased by a spectacle, perhaps, that tends toward pattern. I find I enjoy knowing a bird by its shape, its call, its flight pattern, its preferred roost, its bobs and struts, the tics and quirks that give it a composite personality. Like the ornithologist I am interested—but only mildly—in where it goes, what it eats, how it nests, what it flees from, how it dies and gets reborn. Like the quantity buff I am delighted to add a new species, but if I knew how many I could recognize, the number wouldn't compare with anything. For what I value most is the image that survives the bird's absence.

I love, for instance, to wake by an open window outside Phoenix and hear the desert, throat by throat, come alive. The quail, which have been restless all night, venture a few tentative clucks, and I can picture them like dowagers shuffling among the oleanders. The curve-billed thrasher gives one lewd upward whistle, then lets loose with nonstop gibberish like a crazed auctioneer. Daylight is launched. Cackling, warbling, chattering, cooing and screeching, cries thicken, overlap, diminish and return, and as I lie with my eyes half closed I can single them out. The sad phrase of the dove brings back childhood summers in Wisconsin. The reedy screams of the flickers evoke their arrogant stance on a saguaro, or their flight in swoops and peaks like phone wires seen from a train. Still cruder is the rattle of the cactus wren, whose love call is more like the fart of a tin soldier. The chitter of house finches reminds me of my mail-order bird caller, my shame-faced childhood slinking through suburban back yards. The breathless jabber of the mockingbird distinguishes itself from the thrasher by repeating each riff two or three times, and the vision of its deadly swoop with a flash of wing bars brings back that splendid description in *Pilgrim at Tinker Creek* in which Annie Dillard concludes that "beauty and grace are performed whether or not we will or sense them. The least we can do is to be there." This is the most elegant of birdwatching, to lie with your eyes closed and let the images and associations drift in and out of mind to the music of chance. I understand now why I like to birdwatch. It is to populate the world, or my version of the world, with friends.

Like any passionate concern, birdwatching reaches toward life in the main, but on its own terms. One sees a stiff-legged little brown oval bouncing up the granite, spots it for a rock wren and says, "I know you," because one has seen other rock wrens just like it. One grows attached to a particular hummingbird nesting just outside the window, wishing the best for its brood, assuming it is always the same mama who returns—but female hummingbirds look so nearly alike that only a trained eye can distinguish between species, let alone individuals. Joseph Campbell has written that for the primitive mind each species is a kind of multiplied individual, related to a mythic Master Animal, and while our relationship has been demystified, the psychology probably still holds. Our domesticated higher mammals seem to be individuals like ourselves, and we project personalities onto birds in cages, but the more a creature retreats into the wild, the more it melts for us into a composite personality—which is its myth for us. One of the ironies of birdwatching is that, for all its apparent sentiment, it is rigorously impersonal.

The only individual involved, in fact, is the observer, who may ultimately find himself the most curious observation. I note that the little boy who took down his feeder for lack of novelty and an annoyance with blue jays, has become the adult whose binoculars weigh on his neck if he doesn't see some action. Birdwatching is a test of patience, and I have found how far mine is from that of an ornithologist, let alone a saint. But it is encouraging to note that if a cottonwood is stilled in a rare lapse of wind, one's eyes go straight to the verdin quivering like one restless leaf; or that staring at a tangle of willows I can spot the brown towhee hopping among the stems. Lack of patience is compensated by the fact that our vision has evolved to pick up the faintest stir, the least exception to immobility, and we are inevitably drawn to what action there is. By strange indirection birds are mirrors in which we catch, in passing, our own eyes.

The world of birds, like music, baseball or gin, can sift its way through a personality. Just as most people have sex lives, so do a few have bird lives. Briefly sighted, flashing out of sight, birds are bits of a puzzle we put together a little faster than it unravels. Spontaneous within limits we can recognize, birds help our eyes master the unknown. Wherever this rootless century sends us, we can begin to reorient ourselves through the common language that shares our air: like weather and sky, birds are a frame of reference. A more progressive referent might be rock bands, fast food or TV. But for some of us who are turning down the volume, it is, mercifully, still birdsong.

Bruce Berger

Beyond Full-throated Ease

Springtime in the desert, when insomnia is in full flower—and it isn't just that Arizona, perverse in so many ways, refuses to go on Daylight Saving Time. One could adapt to a day that breaks, cackling, at 4:30 a.m. if it followed some semblance of night. Instead, during the brief, precious hours of darkness, a mockingbird turns the nearest oleander into a bandshell.

By day the bird is possible to tune out, and at nightfall it lapses with other birds into a promising silence. To the mockingbird it is only a snooze, for as soon as you have plunged into your REM sleep you are roused by restored jubilance proclaiming *pierce, pierce, spear, spear, cheaper, cheaper, cheaper, fever, fever, tsk, tsk, tsk, squeegee, squeegee, jeer, jeer, whadja eat, whadja eat, earache, earache, earache,* plus a fervent reserve of rattles, whistles, and jammed starters that defy orthography. I switch on my so-called white noise machine, a little plastic cylinder that emits a whirring sound capable of masking distant dogs while keeping you awake in its own right, and the mockingbird burns through it like an ambulance. Each riff is repeated at least twice, with favorites getting four or five hits, all in such quick succession that the bird at first seems endlessly inventive. After a couple of weeks you realize that there are probably no more than forty distinguishable calls, each one sordidly familiar. Keats's nightingale sang with "full-throated ease." How characteristic that America's nocturnal counterpart knows no such restraint.

While mockingbirds probably don't vary much from

place to place or year to year, one always develops a special, particularized hatred for the individual that has staked one's aural field. This must be the most impassioned jabberwocky of all. As a bird lover it makes me uneasy to imagine this bird through the cross-hairs of a serious silencer, and until recently I hadn't advanced beyond lobbing ornamental oranges and shaking his tree. Suddenly it occurred to me I possessed a more interesting weapon: a tape recorder.

The recording of birds for experiment, identification, and study is now a major pursuit for both ornithologists and hobbyists. Only my motive varied slightly. It was too much to ask that the bird recognize his own nonsense and leave out of embarrassment, but he just might take the playback for another male that had staked his territory, and move on. I set the machine under the bird's favorite palm and punched *Record*. The bird ran through his score. Now and then he flew to an alternate perch fifty feet away and I had to punch *Stop*, but within an hour I had a full side. I rewound and punched *Play*.

B*ruce* B*erger*

At full pitch the recorder was feeble compared to the live bird, which rhapsodized unchecked. In a rare break the beak closed and the tape, pathetically, went *fever, fever*. The bird went *fever, fever*. The tape went *cheaper, cheaper*. The bird lost itself in peals of gibberish, then caught the tape going *tsk, tsk. Tsk, tsk* went the mockingbird.

Several evenings in succession I played the mockingbird back to himself, brandishing the tape as he flitted from tree to tree. My physical presence was, as usual, no deterrent. Occasionally the bird sang in canon with the tape—mocking himself—but mostly he soloed unperturbed. If the bird did consider the tape another male, he probably figured it for a wimpy specimen of little importance. Or perhaps the tape merely short-cut certain song loops. In any case, my arm and my ear soon tired of our duet for one. I might have succeeded with a more virile tape recorder, but I gave up and called the doctor. Local

doctors have mockingbirds of their own, know well why
Phoenix is called the Valley of the Dalmane, and are more
than willing to prescribe little capsules that reach inside the
listener and punch *Stop*.

The
Telling
Distance

Bird's Eye View

When birds catch our attention, it is usually for their commanding dress, their pronouncements, their diverting tics, the sleights of wing that keep them aloft. They seem wary of our interest and prefer to remain in motion, just beyond focus, and unless we trap them in cages, feeders, or binoculars, we very seldom look them in the eye.

Bruce
Berger

To do so is slightly unsettling—as demonstrated by two species common to the Sonoran Desert. By human projection the curve-billed thrasher is an aggressive and feisty robin-sized bird with a sharp, downward-curving bill; abrupt and jerky of movement, vocally raucous and obsessive, it is further damned by its sheath of dull, uniform grey. The only bit of color, in fact, is in the eyes, which through binoculars turn into flat, brilliant, perfectly round, perfectly expressionless disks of topaz, with tiny pupils like fathomless wells. The phainopepla, by contrast, seems gentle and light-hearted, slightly smaller than the thrasher, glossy black, with a jaunty jaylike crest. It eats and distributes the seeds of the mistletoe that grow on palo verdes, and flits from tree to tree flycatcher-fashion, un-programmed as a butterfly, flashing white on its wings, its voice an oboe that asks, over and over, the same wistful question. The sole splash of color in this black and white arrangement is, again, the eye, this one a translucent red bead like a ripe currant. What is disturbing about the ruby and the topaz is that for all the seeming personality of the birds in which they are set, our inspection falls, with a kind of vertigo, into the central black point that expresses only an unvarying, unreadable, merciless awareness.

The eyes of birds have been studied nearly as thoroughly as their ability to fly, and their adaptations seem nearly as oblique. Eyes are the largest structure in a bird's head, and in certain species a pair of them weighs more than the brain. In man the area of greatest visual concentration, known as the fovea, has 200,000 visual cells per square millimeter. Certain hawks have one million cells per square millimeter in their foveae. Birds can see sharply at both shorter and longer distances than man, combining properties of the microscope and telescope, and special muscles refocus from near to far almost instantaneously. The irises of birds have both rods, for night vision, and cones, for daylight and color. Thus equipped, birds have the best vision of any known life form.

Intricate depths adjust the jeweled surfaces. Most of the bird's eye is buried in an unusually large bony hollow known as the sclerotic ring. Within this cavern the eye is rigidly fixed, a grip countered by the flexibility of the neck: man has seven cervical vertebrae, while birds have up to twenty-five, with an average of fourteen. Iris and pupil alone are visible. Expressions that humans shade by reshaping the whites of their eyes—those whites that, exposed at all, give wild looks to horses and dogs—are lacking in birds.

What the world looks like, peering *out* through this apparatus, can be constructed intellectually but never humanly imagined. Eyes of birds are situated on opposite sides of the head, so that there is little or no overlap of vision and the bird sees two fields at once. The bird thus interprets the world through two foveae, two points of focus, surrounded by mists of peripheral vision. Falcons and owls can look straight ahead and focus in three dimensions, more or less as we do, given that falcons see better at a distance and owls better at night. Hawks have a fovea on each side and a third in the middle where the fields of their eyes overlap, so that they coordinate three regions of brilliant focus at once. Robinson Jeffers spoke of the "hawk's realist eye," but what is real for the hawk would be surreal, and sublimely dizzying, for us.

There are, most teasing of all, the anomalies. Some birds bob continuously up and down and it is thought that the two perspectives, the top and the bottom of the bob, are perceptually fused so as to give depth of vision in each eye. Kiwis are nearly blind. And birds have a separately evolved eyelid, known as the nictitating membrane, which is semi-transparent and passes obliquely across the eye from the bill to the ear. The nictitating membrane cleanses the eye and protects it from wind, glare and, in the case of diving birds, from water.

These facts have been marshalled in a stumped attempt to find out what it might mean to walk into the Sonoran Desert and confront the topaz of the thrasher or the ruby of the phainopepla—brilliant attentions one meets without, in the fuller sense, meeting them at all. Why these sharp, improbable colors? Why, for that matter, the dull eye of the robin? Experts who have plumbed optical mechanics, forced to mention the brilliant irises that may have drawn us to their findings, only offer that the eyes are colored "for display purposes" or "for functions unknown." As the anatomists seem to fall, with the rest of us, into the pupils' black hole, they do emit two curious facts. By closing their nictitating membranes, birds are the only creatures that can, if they choose, look directly at the sun. And birds are the only creatures that close their eyes when they die.

Bruce Berger

Fear in the Lower Sonoran

"The desert has claimed another victim," crows the news team whenever the rescue crew arrives too late, or one of our species is found bleaching in a far arroyo. The desert has inspired enough bad press, earned or otherwise, that the human desert rat keeps his head. He carries enough water, or heads to a dependable source. He wears a hat and sensible shoes. Aware how land forms mock each other, he keeps track of his route. He learns how to walk without getting stabbed by cactus and yucca, and avoids tight drainages in dark weather. He knows that the spangle of cottonwoods means water, and that the presence of doves means that it will probably be above ground where he can get at it. He masters his fear of the word *desert* by learning to read the place it stands for.

The desert is in some ways the least mysterious of landscapes. Because of its very dryness, vegetation is well-spaced, visible in the round, and everything lives—or seems to live—in the open. The stillness is not necessarily silent. Birds are more raucous than their forest cousins, and shrieking woodpeckers, cackling quail, chattering thrashers, rattling cactus wrens, and chittering swifts turn dawns and dusks into an amiable madhouse. When wind stirs an oasis, so leathery are the leaves that the ear can break the sound into separate collisions. Visibility often extends for miles. Once its measure has been taken, the desert doesn't threaten; it reassures.

The desert reassures, that is, in the long view. Anyone who has hiked an arroyo in Southern Arizona knows that, moment by moment, one's advance is not so predictable. Doves burst from the trees with their wings squeaking. Quail blow up at your feet. Cottontails and jackrabbits bolt at a dead hobble. Lizards scurry into dry leaves like invisible fire. With clenched heart you launch a coyote's airy bounce, or a javelina's thundering panic. Every desert creature seems to rely on protective coloring until you are on top of it, then goes off in your face. Familiarity comes almost immediately to the rescue, and you learn to identify these explosions within milliseconds. But unlike the threats one prepares for, each burst of sound, no matter how repetitious, is a fresh little scare, a new shot of adrenaline. And in that flick of inner free-fall before the outburst is decoded, another image flashes from the unconscious. The shape is almost invariable from person to person, and lies coiled in the most seasoned desert traveler. It is the fiend in the paradise. Snakes.

Bruce
Berger

In his book of pop ethnology, *The Naked Ape*, Desmond Morris claims that of the twenty most dreamt-of objects, the only animal to make the list is not the domestic dog or cat; it is the snake—a tenacity he ascribes to the danger snakes posed to our arboreal ancestors. Racial memory or not, the persistence of that split-second ghostly image holds equally for those who admire snakes, like myself, and those who regret them, like half of my friends. Oddest among the latter are the many snake-haters who are less afraid of the actual creature than of the *idea* of the snake. They dread most that psychic paralysis when image hits retina, and what they really dread is not the snake but a constriction in their own flesh. Fear feeds on anticipation, breeding odd behavior. One fellow desert rat refuses to go first, even though he believes that the first man will probably rouse the snake in time to bite the second. "After you, snakebait," he says jauntily whenever we set off.

I enjoy snakes enough to pursue them for a second look—yet snakes are the only factor that makes me nervous about hiking the desert alone. I somehow feel that if

I twist an ankle or snap a back, I will crawl to civilization. But if I am envenomed? I have read the statistics reporting that more people are killed annually by honey bees than by snakes, that only three percent of those bitten by rattlers succumb, and that most fatalities are small children. But the same authorities warn you against hiking the desert alone, and that makes me uneasy. I stay in the open where snakes can spot me first, or sense my heat, and carry the stave of a dead saguaro to tap ahead of me over ledges and swish through grass that conceals me from snake level. Less rationally I carry a snakebite kit, but have a block against understanding the instructions and will probably spend my first stricken moments rereading them if I am panicked into using it. I have also read that more people die of infections from self-applied remedies than from the actual venom, and hope that if the worst happens I will stay sane and trust my own antibodies. I will take every precaution except staying home.

Despite our grand obsession, most of the desert's sudden noises are *not* snakes; they are perfectly harmless doves, cottontails, lizards, and mice. The few snakes one does see are usually drab, nondescript little specimens only a herpetologist could adore. But about once a year, despite all precautions, I am rattled at. Far more often the wind blows a seed pod, or I step on dry grass, and I *think* I am rattled at. That first flick of dry sound, snake or not, shoots ice through the marrow—and raises a curious point. Rattlesnakes are purely a New World phenomenon and I am, to my knowledge, of strictly Old World stock. To what threat am I reacting? Were rattlesnakes once more widely diffused? Did some similar sound once threaten elsewhere? Did rattlers infest Pangeia? This knowing jab of terror through newcomers to the hemisphere is a matter I've never seen raised in the literature, let alone answered. At the moment, of course, I'm not faulting the literature but looking for the snake. So effective is the coloration that the snake may remain hidden, but once I have spotted him

I veer smartly toward where the snake is not. Confrontation defused, my pulse calmed and my head cleared, I watch from a fascinated distance, or even pursue him until he disappears. Glad to have cheated the news team, I proceed on my foolish way.

The desert, more than most habitats, shows its creatures full-figure, and the snake is its least popular member. Logically one knows that snakes are part of the balance, keep down the rodent population, and are of scientific value; morally one recognizes their equal right to be here. Even those who find them unesthetic must admit they add to the planet's diversity. But the true desert rat must confess, beyond abstractions, that part of the desert's intensity is its ability to startle, its constant succession of nudges and jabs that keeps you glued to the present. Because the snake sheds its skin, in many mythologies it represents renewal, the ever recurring moment: and when that symbol coils before you in the incarnation of a roused diamondback, there is little division of focus. To play St. Patrick and drive away the snakes could ease one's mind—and rob the desert of its caffeine. The snake may no longer invoke the devil himself, but he reminds us of one of life's great premises—that there is always a present tense one can't quite prepare for.

Bruce Berger

Chimera

There is little so unnerving as a new creature on home ground—and I felt possessive of the miniature cut through one end of the McDowell Mountains, just outside Phoenix. Sporting an occasional pothole, offering few novelties, its chief merit was to lie only twenty minutes from suburbia, just obscure enough that on weekdays one could get there without running a gauntlet of trail bikes and recreational gunslingers.

On the Wednesday in question I took off my clothes except for socks and sneakers, stuffed them into my daypack and scrambled the length of the arroyo, enjoying a semi-athletic soak in the May sun. I reached the far end without incident and started back. My mind probably wandered to some manuscript or other. Suddenly there was a volcanic burst from the hanging foliage of a nearby ironwood, and a frantic scramble up a slope. In the rush of speculation that rides adrenaline, I envisioned a creature too small for a deer and too dense for a coyote. Then I found myself being glared at from beside the tree by an apparition that seemed half head, perhaps two feet tall, razor-backed, gristly, grey, surpassingly ugly. Its noisy companion was still bolting uphill. I knew vaguely that there were such things as wild pigs, imagined they somehow inhabited Mexico or Central America or literary islands, and never expected to confront one within the smog zone of Phoenix. And I was wildly ignorant. Did they attack? Was I about to be turned into savage bacon? Such anarchy surged through me in the time it took me to be ambushed, exchange a wild look and continue walking, unmolested, trying desperately to step normally and not smell like fear.

I have seen javelina numerous times since, and have read enough about them to know they are named for their javelin-like upper canines, and will use them only when unexpectedly cut off from water, offended during rutting season or panicked by coming upon them suddenly—all occasioned by their being still more near-sighted than I. But I will always see the javelina as a chimera exploding from my own fright, escaped to tell me who is the real apparition.

Bruce
Berger

Corralling the Tumbleweed

F or several generations tumbleweed has been a symbol of the open West, the social outcast, the solitary spirit, the romantic loner. An era of beery-eyed dude ranchers has crooned "Tumblin' Tumbleweed" before heading back to the structured East. In vintage Westerns a few tumbleweed propelled by wind machines are *de rigueur*, and most classic is the single specimen that whirls left to right and back left in the background of *Petrified Forest* while Leslie Howard romances the young Bette Davis. And even today someone will drawl over your CB radio, "Breaker, breaker, this is Tumbleweed . . ."

It comes as a shock to learn that tumbleweed is an alien and a subversive. The first seeds are believed to have arrived in a shipment of flax seeds from Russia to North Dakota in 1873. In Russia it was a well-known pest, and it found our prairies as agreeable as the bleak and wind-blown steppes, fanning throughout the Great Plains and the West from sea level to 8,500 feet. By 1895 the Department of Agriculture pronounced it a blight in sixteen states.

If tumbleweed had not arrived so casually one might suspect biological warfare. It flourishes in vacant lots, pastures, roadsides, overgrazed ranges, river bottoms and fallow fields. It loves and encourages poor soil. Piled up against fences it becomes a fire hazard. It plugs culverts, replaces gardens, clogs irrigation ditches and canals. It blows onto highways and diverts drivers into each other. With rare generosity it distributes the sugarbeet leafhopper, which curdles the greens of sugar beets and attacks tomatoes, spinach and beans. In Willa Cather's "Neighbor Rosicky" it takes over an alfalfa field and provokes a fatal heart attack in the story's protagonist, who tries to rake it out. Tumbleweed is about as congenial to fellow plants as the starling is to indigenous songbirds.

Redeeming virtues are marginal. The seeds are edible to rodents and a few birds. In desperate times the young greens can be fed in quantity to cattle, or served mature if cut with the seeds of other plants. Decorators spray them bright colors for those conversation pieces that leave you speechless, and a favored few have been turned into Christmas trees. And drivers who spare their fellow motorists can savor the splash of teased-up shredded wheat.

Formally but inaccurately known as Russian thistle, tumbleweed is not a thistle at all but belongs to the goosefoot family. It begins modestly as a dull cluster of serrated purplish green spikes lost between mallow, saltbush, sage—anything similarly undiscriminating. Visually it already bristles, but only as summer approaches does it begin to bloat, swelling until its airy maze is three feet high and four feet wide, occasionally topping six feet. Midsummer brings its tiny, almost tundra-like white flowers, each with a tinier blood-drop in the center, unnoticed among the leaves. Each flower engenders a single seed. The plant dries, the roots break from the ground and tumbleweed begins to travel in the least puff of wind, strewing an estimated 50,000 to 100,000 seeds. Few of those seeds take root, but at those odds few need to. "Pledging their love to the ground," says the song, and if by love we mean the perpetuation of the species, the lyric is botanically sound.

State and federal agencies spend millions of our tax dollars every year trying to curb tumbleweed. Controlled burning prevents pile-ups from starting fires and loners from cruising the highway. Fields and roadsides are sprayed with poisons, with the usual toxic side-effects. More

Bruce
Berger

imaginatively, in 1974 the *Coleophera parthenica,* an insect from Pakistan that eats tumbleweed, was introduced near Indio, California, and subsequently in several other states. The larvae crawl up the branches, eat, hatch into egg-laying moths, and cripple the plant's capacity to produce seeds. It has been determined that the *Coleophera parthenica* eats *only* tumbleweed, and will presumably disappear after it has dispatched its ubiquitous host. Other researchers, assuming tumbleweed will survive imported bugs, are attempting to put the plant to good use. Biotechnologists at New Mexico State University are trying to manipulate tumbleweed genetics so that a single plant will bear twelve varieties of desert flowers. More plausibly, the Office of Arid Land Studies at the University of Arizona is deliberately growing tumbleweed on exhausted farmland, harvesting it with cotton farming equipment, and compacting it into Tumblelogs, a fireplace fuel they hope will prove more economical than other synthetic logs on the market. So far the plant looks impervious to insect, poison, and inventor.

As a personality the wayward tumbleweed is more than a romantic rambler; it is a bristling, self-enclosed, solipsistic maze, a single continuous shoulder shrugging the world aside. As with so many of our myths, the debunking of a colorful, free-wheeling countryman leaves one a little disheartened. But in an age so divorced from its emblems that patriotic citizens can trap, shoot and poison our National Bird, there is no reason to fear the loss of a symbol if truth or the *Coleophera parthenica* wins out. The myth of the West is proving still tougher than the West itself, and if all else fails we can watch the old pest in reruns on TV, or sing along with all those space-loving dude ranchers who have gone west to stay.

A Mist on Stilts

A watercolorist wishing to capture tamarisk would moisten the paper with a wash of soft grey. With the paper half dry he would float on the pastels—muted green for the foliage, cream to pale lilac for the late spring flowers, curry and saffron for the changes of mid-fall. When the colors were entirely dry he would add a few slashes of burnt sienna, underneath and among the branches, for a trunk and a suggestion of stems. And there, with luck, his tamarisk would stand: an explosion of cobweb, a mist on stilts. For a tamarisk is a living watercolor, and it is that medium, letting white paper sing through the colors, that can best conjure the illusion of stopped smoke.

Like the tumbleweed, tamarisk is so much a part of the Western scene that many landscapes would seem graceless without it, yet it too is not native. Its scale-like leaves, more like sprays of soft needles, led to its being named from *tamarik*, Hebrew for cleanliness, presumably because it was used as a broom. Centuries back the plant spread from its home in the Jordan Valley throughout the Arab world and the countries that ring the Mediterranean. The first specimens probably arrived in this country soon after the turn of our century, though Willa Cather, ever the novelistic botanist, places them perhaps anachronistically in the adobe villages of Arizona and New Mexico in *Death Comes for the Archbishop*, set in 1858, and calls them "the tree of the people . . . like one of the family in every Mexican household." In any case farmers found them useful as

Bruce Berger

windbreaks in fields, the Southern Pacific Railroad planted them extensively in sandy areas to help stabilize tracks, ranchers cut them into furniture and fence posts, and their first uses were more likely functional than decorative.

But tamarisk today is less a stabilizer and an ornamental than a weed. Thriving through salt, heat, wind and drought, it is almost indestructible once established. Its tough, fiber-like roots weave a tight labyrinth just below the surface, sending up shoots only inches apart, growing up to fifteen feet a year, launching jungles in a single season. Its cycle is so timed that seeds are released during high water, then left conveniently stranded as rivers recede and reservoirs are drawn down. It spreads less like a plant than a disease. Almost every watercourse in the desert is colonized by tamarisk, and I particularly treasure an idyllic side canyon where it has been unable to clear a hurdle of pools and waterfalls, a hide-out which shall go unnamed lest the pest learn to read.

Most of tamarisk's virtues are vices in disguise. Nothing will grow in their deep shade, where bits of shed foliage heap up like All-Bran. Their litter will stain anything parked beneath, and in urban areas they act as a filter for dust—only to release it all at once in a good burst of wind. Named for cleanliness, tamarisk are nonetheless considered a "messy" tree. Hikers and river runners nurse the scars of their impassable thickets. Their stabilizing roots, meanwhile, gulp quantities of water that formerly sustained native plants, and their vice-like attack can sever pipes, sewer lines, septic tanks—anything that comes between them and a drink. It is too bad that no one thought to drop a few seeds into the wet cement as Glen Canyon Dam was being built, or that great lost canyon system might have been saved for still more tamarisk—and ourselves.

What we call tamarisk, for good or for ill, is actually a species with seventy-five varieties worldwide, twelve of them on the loose in the United States. The huge ornamentals in cities, up to forty feet high with trunks that would do credit to an elm, are seldom found by the riverside. Our sandbars are graced with a smaller French variety, nicknamed salt cedar not only because it grows in saline soil but because it actually gives off salt from cells in its leaves and flowers. Salt builds up until the plant appears to be rising from a white shadow. A subspecies of salt cedar produces a salt which is sugary, and which speculation has linked to the Biblical manna.

Speculation has also linked the Hopis to the lost tribes of Israel, but the hard news is that tamarisk is here to stay. Their monoculture has replaced willows, reeds and numberless native plants on which local animals, insects and birds were dependent. Yet doves manage to nest in the branches, roadrunners lay their eggs underneath and honey bees find them nutritious. I have seen at least five species of insects buzzing frantically about the trees in mid-autumn, well after blooming season. In the fullness of time—if we don't diminish the West still further—tamarisk may become part of a well-rounded, stable, altered but complex new system.

Already tamarisk is part of the Western mood. In a land of hard edges they bloom between water and rock like clouds of doubt. In the brightest sun they refuse to focus, and to wander among them on a wet cloudy day, in heavy dew or after a rain has weighted their plumes with lugubrious drops, is to stroll through a stanza of Poe. Tamarisk, in a sense, was the first Mid-Eastern takeover, and like tumbleweed, that Mongol invader, it has proved the world botanically a global village before Marshall McLuhan gave us the phrase. Tamarisk may be a pest, but it is a beautiful pest, part of the West's richness, and firmly entrenched—so we might as well break out our watercolors and adapt. We are, most of us, newcomers to this continent ourselves.

*Bruce
Berger*

The Mysterious Brotherhood

It was a custom in medieval times for saints and scholars to keep a human skull around to remind them of their mortality. That practice seems morbid as we plunge, youth-obsessed, toward the twenty-first century, and the great bonescapes of Georgia O'Keeffe, their elegant folds of calcium and sky, remind us less of death than the deep cleanliness beneath the flesh. To see finality as a kind of radiance, one can turn to the desert not just for the melodramatic bones—which, despite cartoons, are few and far between—but for the quieter revelations of the vegetable world. Those unlikely green lives, each stranded in its claim to water, shed their skins to reveal still deeper miracles.

Cactus are among our most treasured species, yet only cholla has attained posthumous notoriety. The cuddly looking shrubs—actually great fountains of barbed grenades which, in certain varieties, nearly leap out for affection—strew in death the sections of their hollow stems, lattices of holes strung together by a woody fiber like asbestos. The delicacy of the recurrent patterns, the modulations of their holes, their rich patina make them sought after, and they grace the kinds of coffee tables where manhattans are served, find their way into flower arrangements, are positioned as a foil for foliage. They have been strung into lamps, hung up as hat racks, woven into macrame, tricked out as toy covered wagons. They have been stood on end and hollowed with ovals for the insertion of Heidi vignettes in isinglass, seashells and mother of pearl. They have in fact been conscripted for so many forms of kitsch, schlock and inventive bad taste that they seem some Sonoran revenge on deer antlers, abalone shells and Japanese fishing balls.

But it would be too bad to let their abuse obscure one of the desert's most moving cycles. Even as the cholla grows it drops its extremities, and if the pieces are not dispersed by wind, water, the flanks of animals or your pierced skin, they mass themselves under the plant like a field of charcoal. As the plant ages, the trunk turns black, the needles become brittle and the skin begins to peel. The cholla may simply crumble, strewing bits of its stem among the decayed pieces, or tip intact into a small jungle gym. But if it remains on its feet, stripped to its fretted skeleton, it leaves a shape refined as sculpture, lord of its clearing, elegant by day and a spidery presence beneath the moon.

The prickly pear, less noble than the cholla, simply runs out of strength and lays its pads on the ground. If it is noticed at all, it seems a vaguely repellent grey heap. Trodden upon it answers crisply to the shoe, a sensuous crunch like a bite of water chestnut or the slow dismemberment of a champagne cork. The serenity of its depths can call up visions of snakes napping in the cool, scorpions at rest, tarantulas digesting their friends. Menacingly pale, it is most comfortably crossed after making a fair noise, in a state of high alertness. "Here we go round the prickly pear," said T. S. Eliot, and one can see why.

But reach down and examine a pad. The skin, turned sulphurous brown, peels off like cracked cardboard, to reveal a mesh of fibrous sheets, each stamped with a similar pattern like a netting of veins and arteries, laminated sheet onto sheet. Each layer is a faint variation on the last as the holes rework their shapes throughout the pad. Fat green health hides the complexity of the prickly pear, and its disclosure is one of death's small rewards.

The smaller the cactus, the denser its spines, until one

reaches the pincushion, one to three inches high, a white thimble usually nestled beneath some larger plant. The pincushion reverses the process by dying inside out, the flesh collapsing to leave a standing cup of barbed lace. Seldom recognized, the spent pincushion is a strange jewel, a crucible of woven stars each sprouting a hook like a talon, delicate as a doll's negligee.

Death on the desert: its forms are extravagant as the species themselves—the barrel's great mashed thumb, the organ pipe's burnt candelabra, the staghorn still more like antlers when stripped of its flesh. But for sheer pageantry the saguaro remains supreme. Largest of the cactus except for its Mexican cousin, the *cardón*, the saguaro reveals itself by painful degrees, breathtakingly. "What will become of . . . the huge and delicate saguaro?" asks Richard Shelton in his moving poem, "Requiem for Sonora," but delicacy would not seem a prime characteristic of this stout colossus, one of whose arms, even as I watch in a suburban backyard, has been severed for months, is dangling by a thread, and is blooming furiously. The saguaro can be killed, *is* being killed by destruction of habitat, but the individual, capable of storing up to ten tons of water, taking fifteen years to grow the first foot, surviving a half century before it blooms and attaining a height of sixty feet, seems resilient to an inspiring degree.

We know when an animal like ourselves dies: it is the moment when the heart stops beating. But when does a plant die? When it turns brown? When it falls? When the shape is finally obliterated? The saguaro begins to die even as it grows. King of its habitat, it is home to entire species of woodpeckers and flickers, which riddle it with holes for many other varieties of birds. The injured pulp secretes a thick shell, a petrified leather that offers a comfortable cave for the nesting bird while protecting the cactus, a hole that actually survives the plant in a collectible object called a desert boot. Branches routinely meet with calamity, suffer injury or fall off, to shrivel like crocodiles in the sun, yet the plant grows on, oblivious. The more grotesque its deformities, the more humanly it seems to express itself. By maturity the plant is pocked, gouged, may be missing or trailing branches, or gored to its bare ribs as if it were being eaten by darkness. Remorselessly it thrives. By the time it is actually ready to die, at the age of one hundred fifty or two hundred years, the saguaro may seem the butt of assaults past imagining.

At last letting go, the energy-collecting green skin turns sallow: the plant's least attractive phase. After preliminary jaundice the outer skin deepens, hardens, begins to crinkle, and finally attains a kind of rich parchment. It extrudes a shiny black substance sticky to the eye, glassy as obsidian to the touch, as if it were being caramelized. Peeling skin reveals the inner pulp turning black, a burnt coral brittle to probing fingers. When tapped the skin now gives a report like a primitive drum, and could almost be played like a xylophone. Itself in sepia, the entire saguaro appears to be burning from inside.

At last the flesh is fallen, the skin strewn like old vellum, and the saguaro stands revealed: a white idea. If the specimen has many branches, or the ribs extend too far, the extremities will sheer off, leaving stumps in a variety of crosses and elemental shapes. Occasionally a cactus boot, former home of some flicker or owl, will catch in the ribs, a hole become substance, revealed as if in a structural model. Tough skin at the bottom may hold the freed ribs like poles in an umbrella stand, an immense rattle when shook. But at last the saguaro will fall. It is now only a confusion of hard skin, spines and crumpled flesh, with perhaps a stray boot, though even now the flung ribs may parody its shape in split bamboo.

Object of beauty, toy, curiosity, decoration, cheap firewood, musical instrument, home for scorpions, motive for metaphor—even a dead cactus has its uses. But a taste for the desert is a taste for ultimates, and death is the backdrop against which all we know comes to brilliance.

Bruce
Berger

Cactus tell us nothing of what's ahead, any more than the death of a close friend: all they reveal is process, but process which retains, even in human terms, immeasurable beauty. Their odd green lives, if nothing else, bring to consciousness our complicity in a mystery that becomes, even as we reject it, our own:

> Saguaros brave putrefaction like tough meat.
> Chollas strew black fruit while a skinful of char
> Peels into moonlight bleaching on its feet.
> The ocotillo collapses into a star.
> A mesh of fiber loosened by your nail
> Separates into bones of the prickly pear.
> Or lay your hands on a lung. Resemblances fail.
> Death is a common bond we never share.

The
Telling
Distance

PURSUIT AND FLIGHT

Surviving the Breaks

"May I have one of the pottery fragments to keep?"
"Anything you like, but don't burn your hands."

I went back outside, to the firepit where Nathan Youngblood had just attempted to fire a red plate in his mother's backyard. A grey heap of shrapnel lay strewn near a fire still smouldering. I touched a plate gingerly; the December twilight had turned it cold as the ground. Sifting among the pieces I found one slightly larger than the rest, like rough sandstone on one side, on the other side a glossy brick red bearing a cup-shaped impression with three flecks like apostrophes across the cup's top—one of four bear-paw designs that had been ranged like compass points around the plate's perimeter. A ceramic representing many hours' work and destined to be sold for many hundreds of dollars had just blown up, but I was pleased with my remnant.

This routine disaster was the culmination of a two-day attempt to fire pottery at the Santa Clara Pueblo between Christmas and New Year's, an inauspicious time. The firing of ceramics out in the elements rather than in a kiln is always precarious, because the least wind can ambush the fire, heat one side of the pottery more than another, and set it off like a land mine. Even on the long still days of summer, a sudden breeze can blow up a pot. But shows and galleries now demand work from the top ceramicists all year, contracts must be met, and traditional pottery must be fired at untraditional times.

When I arrived in northern New Mexico the day before, to watch this last stage of pottery-making, the weather was socked in. "Do you really think you can fire now?" I asked Nathan Youngblood.

"It's supposed to clear tomorrow. Today I'll build a fire in the pit and dry out the ground. There's been rain and then snow and everything is soaked."

"What difference would wet ground make, if the fire is hot enough?"

"Wet ground causes steam to rise through the fire and cloud the finish on the pottery. Fire that produces shiny work has to be dry."

A tall and muscular man of thirty whose small, studious features belie his sense of humor, Nathan Youngblood lives outside Santa Fe, and drives twenty miles north to the Santa Clara Pueblo, on the outskirts of Española, to fire pottery in his mother's backyard. This part of the pueblo seemed a scrawny suburbia of one-story adobes and wooden frame buildings, arranged in a loose grid with open fields in between. Here and there in neighboring yards stand the conical shapes of kilns—for firing bread, not pottery. Mela Youngblood's yard may look equally undistinguished from a distance, but its contents are curious. An old turquoise boiler sprawls at an odd angle. Projecting from one end of the boiler are four large rectangles of corrugated tin in wooden frames, angled so that walls and boiler form a small corral with a depression in the middle: the firepit. A roof on wooden posts, projecting from the house, shelters piles of wood and a row of metal garbage cans containing various clays. And all about, in cubes and rectangles, lies wire mesh—metal crates that used to hold milk bottles, old wire bicycle baskets, charred oven racks and refrigerator shelves. Iron grillwork over the back windows seems to continue the motif.

Nathan lifted a tarp off the firepit, and a bit of the water it held slipped back into the hole. He asked me to remove the tin wall next to the boiler, then scooped off the top layer of the firepit with a shovel and heaved the ashes

Bruce Berger

through the opening. The ground lay charred for some distance beyond the firepit. "The base of this pit is adobe clay we brought here. It's less permeable than the ground, dries out quicker, and makes a good base for the fire." He split a few pieces of wood with a hatchet and tossed them into the pit. "Cedar," he said. "Splits easily, starts fast, and burns hot." He squirted some fire-starter. "Traditional kerosene," he said, "though usually we rub two sticks together. It's cold. Let's go inside."

Mela Youngblood's small living room was decorated for Christmas, with a tree in one corner and garlands of tinsel looped around Indian baskets that formed a kind of frieze near the ceiling. But what distinguished the room was its profusion of black pottery. Two large black storage jars were filled with poinsettias, and two more had been made into lamps whose shades featured Indian motifs in needlepoint. Most impressive was a display case of works by members of the extended family—small bowls, tiny wedding jars, animal figures that included bears, dogs, even a penguin. A friendly, compact and direct-spoken woman in her fifties, Mela explained what periods the various pieces represented. "But if you really want to see pottery," she said, "follow me."

She led us to a room off the hall in which jars of all sizes loomed out of the darkness. There were storage jars made by her mother, Margaret Tafoya, and jars by Margaret's mother, Serafina. On the floor, looking as if it concealed a body, was a bulging tarp. "This is where I keep my clay," said Mela, poking it with her foot, "though I refuse to do any more work until after the holidays." Here, then, was pottery stretching back four generations, and clay waiting to be fired into new pots. Here was the Santa Clara tradition, in transit.

Santa Clara pottery has, in a sense, two traditions. The older lineage is the slow evolution of fired vessels that can be traced back to the first Pueblo agricultural settlements in the Rio Grande Valley, around 500 A. D. The pottery consisted of assorted storage and cooking jars, and pieces whose use was strictly ceremonial. Incoming Spaniards found Pueblo pottery useful, and actually expanded its production. But the arrival of Anglos in the last century brought machine-made products from the eastern United States and Europe—metal pots, chinaware—eliminating the need to make utilitarian pieces in the old way. The tradition of ceramics guttered without quite dying out, for with the coming of the railroads, tourism, and the advent of collectors who looked on pottery as a branch of esthetics, a new market—and a new tradition—was born. Jars incorporating the old motifs were made for their artistic appeal, and developed into a new style with its roots in the old.

The central figure in the resurgence of Santa Clara pottery is Margaret Tafoya, still potting in her early eighties. It was she who brought to perfection the large storage jars she learned to make from her mother, Serafina. Carved into deep relief by her husband, Alcario, Tafoya jars have become the Santa Clara trademark. Later in her career Margaret specialized also in a more delicate red ware. For Mela, and then for Nathan and his sister Nancy, Margaret was the decisive influence, teacher of a tradition and embodiment of the tradition itself.

Surrounded by black pots, we settled in Mela's living room, where Nathan kept track of some football on TV, slipped out during the breaks to toss more cedar on the fire, and explained how he became involved in pottery. With a father in the military, Nathan and Nancy had lived all over the United States and Europe by the time Nathan was fourteen. After high school in Santa Cruz and college at the University of New Mexico, Nathan wound up working in a restaurant in Santa Fe. When the restaurant closed and he lost his job, Nathan's parents, and Nancy, who had been potting for a couple of years, encouraged him to try the family trade.

It was a difficult apprenticeship, and the best possible,

for Nathan wound up living for nearly two years with his grandmother. Margaret teaches by example rather than direct instruction, and for Nathan it was largely a time when the work came out flawed or broken, full of days when he got disgusted with pottery and quit to fire up some food. It was only gradually, as he turned out his first successes, that he began to enjoy the process itself. It was well that he learned from his grandmother, for unlike his sister, who invents many of her shapes and specializes in miniatures, Nathan had dedicated himself to reproducing many of the larger forms characteristic of the twenties and thirties. "There were so many great shapes back then, pieces that you look at structurally and think, how the hell did they make them! Difficult handles, long sections, very thin pots—those are the shapes I want to reproduce."

With Margaret there were to be no shortcuts. "One of the first things you get from Grandma is a lecture on responsibility, on having respect for the clay. It's like the reverence a lot of potters have for the land. It's not just there to take—you're *allowed* to use it." As Nathan talked and the fire smouldered in the backyard, the clouds slowly lifted, and by the end of the day the Sangre de Cristo Mountains glimmered in the east like a surf of calm whitecaps.

When I got to Mela's the next morning, clouds and patches of snow were still shrinking and Nathan had a new fire started in the pit. It would be mid-afternoon before the coals were steady enough for firing the red plate, as well as a larger jar with six indentations around the base, to be fired black. Meanwhile, in addition to football and conversation there was work to be done, and Nathan sat at the kitchen table sanding the jar over a cardboard box. "In the old days they used wet corn cobs to smooth down the jars," he said, "but this stuff does a much better job." Soon he handed the jars and sandpaper to his mother, and brought out two coffee cans with the slips—red clay suspended in water, to provide coloration. He painted the face of the plate rapidly with a one-inch brush, while Mela painted the jar with the rust-colored slip used for black ware.

After the red was even on the plate, Nathan brought out a small box of polishing stones, mentioning that some had been passed down for generations and others had been bought for a quarter at a rock shop. There was petrified wood, Apache tears, anonymous riverstones—every potter had some odd favorites—but this was a stage Nathan didn't care for: Mela hates shaping but loves polishing, while Nathan hates polishing but loves shaping. He licked the stone and rubbed it on the plate, producing shiny lines that coalesced in a glossy surface, licking and rubbing until his chin was red as if he'd been eating pizza. "Is there any danger from licking that stuff?" I asked.

"As a matter of fact, yes, it can't be good for you. We've tried dipping it in a glass of water instead, but it takes extra time and we just don't do it. But there are hazards at all stages. The place where we get the clay is full of rattlesnakes. We go in October when there are fewest, and no one has been bitten—yet—but we have to be careful. When we dig the volcanic ash for the temper, and when we sift it, the stuff rises like powder and gets in your eyes and nose. A lot of potters develop back problems from lifting heavy things from the fire, which they have to do fast, and my doctor has told me I should take salt tablets before the firing because I sweat so much. That's the least of it with the firing. Even wearing gloves you can burn your hands when you pick up the grill—and you can smell the leather burning. Actually you can tell when someone fires traditionally because of the battle scars—singed hair and eyebrows, burns on their arms. But the worst is what you breathe. A firing turns your mucus black. You'll blow your nose, and black stuff still comes out a week later."

"Can't you wear a mask?"

"We've tried bandannas during the sanding so our sinuses don't flare up, but they're hard to get used to. And we've tried masks during the firing, but we sweat so much they just slide off—they should make them with industrial strength rubber bands!" Nathan paused, shrugged. "But then, we could get nuked any minute."

Nathan checked the surface of the plate "for hoo-ha's," painted a circle of plain water in the middle of the unpainted back, and signed his name in pencil in the wet spot—the last touch before the firing.

In the backyard the coals had sunk to a steady glow, filling the air with a scent like smoky turpentine. Nathan turned the pieces of wood over to make sure all the moisture was out, since that too could dull the finish, and let them burn a little longer. "What are the odds?" I asked.

"Last year I fired twenty pieces for Indian Market, and only two came out. Most of them literally blew up. Sometimes they all come out, and sometimes none of them do. The amount of oxygen is important. If the wind's blowing, it will heat one side quicker than the other, and you overfire one side. That's why we pick windless days whenever possible."

When the overturned coals were burning evenly, Nathan placed four charred tin cans in a square, and set a wire milk carton on top. He set a smaller grill on edge inside so that it rested against two sides of the carton, then stood the plate on its rim, leaning against the grill. He set several thin pieces of tin across the top, forming a solid roof. The plate looked like a caged animal.

"Do you always fire just one at a time?"

"Almost always, except for miniatures, because if one piece blows up it wrecks all the rest. We used to build contraptions where there'd be a bottom grill and separate grills on each side leaning in, and sometimes they'd collapse and scratch the pot. Now we're buying up all the milk cartons and old-time heavy bicycle baskets we can find. When I fire a big piece I have to create a box from the racks of refrigerators and stoves, and wire them into one big cage. When you consider all the time that goes into a large piece, and the price it will sell for, it's silly not to take the time to get everything exactly right."

Nathan placed fresh cedar sticks and newspapers under the carton, crouched and blew on the coals, raising the flame. He set ponderosa bark around all sides of the cage and on top, encasing it in wood, saying that ponderosa was less knotty than other woods, didn't pop, and burned evenly. It was scrap they were able to get from a local lumber mill every November. He poured kerosene around the bark, and flames engulfed the construction, a toy house on fire. The air seemed windless. We stared at the flames with the glazed look induced by all hearths and campfires. "How much longer will you leave it in?" I asked.

There was a crack, as if a firecracker went off, and the ponderosa on my side blew out, sending bark toward my feet and opening a full view of the flames inside. "Not much longer," said Nathan.

Bruce
Berger

We stared, Nathan impassively and myself incredulously, at the crumbled remains. "Probably the clay wasn't dry enough. The plate was four weeks old, which should have been enough to dry it, but who knows in this weather? The jar is newer, so there's no use blowing that one up too."

That meant Nathan wouldn't be performing the extra step that turns the pottery black—the shoveling of dried horse and cow manure onto the fire, reducing the temperature and raising a thick smoke that draws oxygen from the clay, replaces it with carbon, and creates a lustrous black finish. We wouldn't smell what Nathan's sister refers to as "Corral No. 5." After two days of preparation for the firing, and many preceding days on Nathan's part to bring the red plate to the final stage, this was *it*.

As we walked back to the house, the implications of this little misfiring began to dawn on me. Nathan Youngblood has become one of the rising figures in Pueblo pottery, a link in the ongoing tradition. He has won many awards, including Best of Class in several of the annual Indian Markets in Santa Fe, and has commanded top prices in leading galleries. Many of those who buy his works know, in a general way, the painstaking process that produced it. Yet who will remember a short winter day when a red plate blows up? Behind the surviving pieces that command admiration in markets, galleries, museums, and homes, how many fragments, lavished with the same care, lie kicking in the dust?

Other thoughts were of the tradition itself. Much of the hazard might be removed from the process by firing in a kiln—yet even this firing in Mela's backyard had its innovations. Milk bottle crates, bicycle baskets and oven racks were hardly Native American inventions—not to mention sandpaper, paintbrushes, kerosene, and cuttings from the lumberyard. Margaret Tafoya still sifts the clay with her hands, but most younger potters run theirs through a wire mesh. An earlier generation fired pottery on rocks instead of grills, but thought of placing bed-springs between the pots to prevent the accumulation of soot. Before the arrival of the Anglos, innovation arose from trading between tribes, and then with the Spaniards, resulting in the constant incorporation of new materials. Adaptation, and the discovery of new uses for old cast-offs, is as Indian as it is Anglo. Where are all the revolving piano stools? In duck blinds, where hunters wheel and shoot. Where are the wire milk cartons? Getting charred in Indian backyards. What does tradition measure? More precisely, the *degree* of change.

I showed Nathan the bear-paw fragment I'd fished from the wreckage. "Look how you have the surface of the plate," he said, "but the underside is all rough because the back is gone. That shows there was water in the middle, which expanded and blew the plate up."

If this was failure, it was the sort of failure one learns from and builds on, that leads to great work. Failure or not, it felt lucky in my pocket.

Decline of the Desert Dream

Bruce Berger

Ever since Scottsdale, Arizona, swelled from a ranching crossroad to a tourist sieve in the late forties, it has bloomed with galleries dispensing the Desert Dream school of art. Just as Carmel for decades has featured gelatinous combers splashing toward sienna cypresses squeezed hot from the tube, so have the boutiques of Scottsdale burst with stainless arroyos, saguaros like noble sentinels, prickly pears of perfectly poised ovals, sweeps of poppies and desert marigolds and perhaps, for a touch of animation, a roadrunner here or a flock of quail over there. In the background one often met the classic west flank of Superstition Mountain, like a crumbling mansard roof, below which a trail, with or without horse and rider, might vanish around a bend. These classic ingredients, endlessly recombined in oil and watercolor in a spectrum of brush techniques, all gave the same impression: that the desert was always spotless, always in bloom, and nobody ever lived there.

And so the dream has held over the years. But the artist, working from life or his own photographs, has found his raw material harder to come by. Setting up his easel in some arroyo, he automatically screens out the Budweiser cans and shell boxes, the trail bike scars and disposable diapers. He strikes the jet trails from the sky. He blots with palo verdes the housing tracts creeping up the Superstitions. As the drone of far semis and the concussive whap of helicopters singe his ears, the artist adjusts, rearranges, lies to be true to the dream.

But the canvas of the Sonoran Eden has nonetheless changed. In the stark blue sky one detects the breath of charcoal, the incursion of pearl, a band like flannel hugging the horizon. The clouds, once only cumulus billows, are often feathers frayed from a contrail's clean straight edge. A nearby ironwood or saguaro may assume an unjustified prominence, as if screening something foul. Superstition Mountain, shown less often, is now glimpsed through shrubbery that blocks all but a face too steep to build on. As artists have kept the faith, the vision has corroded, darkened, retreated through a gradual scrim. The Scottsdale Eden has corrupted unawares. It is only in a few lodges that haven't been replaced by condominiums, or on a private adobe wall, that a heavily framed canvas will recall the gleaming sand, the deep-shadowed peaks and hot blue sky of the Sonoran dream.

The
Telling
Distance

Brush Fire

After the ranch hands and volunteers have beaten the fire with brooms and wet burlap, after the smoke has ceased and the rangelands of west Texas stretch in bituminous folds, only the yucca stands unscarred with its vibrant green spikes and its stalk of creamy white bloom. Within weeks new grass will push through the volcanic soil, and within months cattle will return for nourishment, but first to arrive is the artist with his paints and his black velvet. Just as the watercolorist achieves effects of snow by letting white paper sing through the brushwork, so does the painter on black velvet leave his medium blank to conjure the burnt fields. Setting his easel before the tough succulent, the artist transcribes the olive spikes and richly flowered stalks of these desert members of the lily family. For the following season, in boutiques, in shopping malls, at roadside stands throughout the West, lovers of arid lands will take strength from the flame-resistant yucca, spending its lone sweetness amid the bullfighters, spaniels and crucifixions.

Bruce Berger

Books on My Back

S omerset Maugham was so addicted to the written word that he carried with him, on his incessant travels, a vast laundry bag stuffed with every sort of volume. Out of great literature, he would settle for catalogs and repair manuals. Reading less for pleasure or edification than out of compulsion, Maugham had a horror of running out of his drug, and his book bag caused strong porters to reel.

The backpacker, as his own beast of burden, cannot support such a habit. We became poor porters when we began to walk upright, and civilization has made us dependent on instant bed and board, water and fire, clothing and the utensils to make it all work. We have become so sophisticated, in fact, that to escape with the bare necessities has become our luxury, and our needs have been duly freeze-dried, compressed, goose-downed and aluminumized to reduce the proportions. But even a backpacker does not live by gorp alone, and there seems no reason not to slip a discreet paperback, or two, among the essentials.

Literati on the brink of a walk must consider two criteria: the book as content and as physical object. Seemingly unrelated, these considerations are less so upon examination. Just as food should be drained of bulk and equipment minimalized, so does language travel better if it is compressed, elegant, trimmed of fat, rich but essential. There is no point in warping one's spine under heaped-up adjectives, wrenched metaphors, massed exposition, stale conclusions and rhetorical froth.

I have backpacked with many books and have found, ounce for ounce, that all but the worst have added far more pleasure than burden. I have indulged a weakness for the novels of Conrad and Durrell, the poetry of Wallace Stevens. I have found the comedies of Shakespeare particularly mobile. The difficult poetry one never quite finds time for can give hours of sport in a few pages, and there is a great freedom, a luxury, in being able to exhaust a chosen passage, or a book, without intervention. It is an opportunity not just to read, but to reread.

And like creatures of the wild, books can behave unexpectedly. I recently packed *Pilgrim at Tinker Creek* on a ten-day hike along the Escalante River, intending to let Annie Dillard's questions about life's extremities hone themselves on the desert—only to find the particulars of the book and the trip running parallel like strands of a double helix. Did Remo mention a close brush with cone-nose bugs? "The cone-nose bug, or kissing bug," reports the book, "bites the lips of sleeping people, sucking blood and injecting an excruciating toxin." Did I remark that the full moon keeps me awake? " 'Some cannot sleep well in a white tent under a full moon,' " Dillard quotes a campcraft authority, adding with amusement, "I like the way that handy woodsy tip threatens us with the thrashings of the spirit." Did Carmen disappear for several hours while we had visions of her being detained by a snake? I picked up the book to distract myself, and read, "I never step foot out of the house, even in winter, without a snakebite kit in my pocket." Were we overwhelmed with ants and bees? Gloria blamed the prevalence of insects on the book's remembered obsessions. One morning I was reading in my sleeping bag, torn between getting up to relieve myself and finishing a chapter. I decided to wrap up the chapter. The next paragraph described the functioning of the kidney. I shot from the bag.

Near the end of the book I was immersed in a scene in which Dillard watches a mosquito sting a copperhead,

Bruce Berger

expressing amazement that insects bite snakes, when Su asked if I would walk with her to the next bend while she tested a newly bandaged toe. On the sandbar at the bend she spotted a small watersnake with a minnow in its mouth. The fish was slightly wider than the snake, and the snake was having a difficult time swallowing. From nowhere a hornet lit on the snake's head and appeared to be biting. The snake drew back as if in pain, heaved and thrashed with the heavy fish, and the hornet flew away. Su, having seen enough, also left. The hornet returned, buzzed the snake's head while the snake shied, then settled near the fish's tail and appeared to feed. I watched as if living the book while hornet and snake dined together, and by the time I left the snake had swallowed half the minnow in a series of backward heaves. I'm glad I wasn't reading *Deliverance*.

It has been objected by purists that literature creates an alternate reality that competes with the real world, dividing the mind and corrupting experience. The primitive virtues are, by definition, pre-Gutenberg, and sharpened attention cannot serve two masters. There is truth to this charge, but it betrays the attitude that literature is essentially an escape from reality rather than a penetration. The choice of book, here, is crucial. Anyone brainless enough to pack a guide to self-improvement, or a novel of urban decay, deserves every schizophrenia. I feel more and more, particularly in the wilds, like Annie Dillard, who says, "I shy away . . . from the human emotional stew. I read what the men with the telescopes and microscopes have to say . . ." One could go so far as to bring a book about the location of one's hike, which might enrich the experience—or might pre-empt original response. Any object packed into the wilderness assumes new importance, and a book that lessens the impact of one's surroundings is indeed an intrusion.

Wilderness is above all an opportunity to heighten one's awareness, to locate the self against the nonself. It is a springboard for introspection. And the greatest words, those which illumine life as it is centrally lived and felt, intensify that process. They provide perspective, a bright mirror that counterpoints and ambushes reality. In isolation one's thoughts can play themselves out without intrusion from the phone, the news media, work, social obligations, conditioned pleasures—or other books. The right writing sharpens, rather than divides, one's perceptions. Somerset Maugham, the quintessential literary traveler, did not miss much of the passing scene.

Such considerations presume an expedition of time, leisure, the indulgence of whim. Survivalists bent on pushing their frames to the limit are better off packing a few extra energy bars. But those bewitched by the written word need not suffer guilt, or attempt withdrawal, merely because they are headed into the bush. It is in isolation that their habit may break into full flower. It is in the sane outdoors that the distilled thought of one's predecessors or one's contemporaries can become, as it should, a strand of the full life.

Cold Pastoral

Silence and slow time out of ancient seabeds, the sandstone heaved into red walls blackened with lichen and rain, stained with the guano of hawks and eagles. Along the canyon floor, clover and tall grasses, cattail, willows, milkweed and rabbit brush extend twin strips of meadow, classically peaceful, and between them flows the Escalante River under the clean blue of the sky. Water is drawn from that sky by the Aquarius Plateau, feeding plants that return year after year, fracturing the rock a little farther along its recurrent seams, in a cycle so timeless as to seem ceremonial. And equally timeless is a pattern in sand along the water's edge, where the pads of mountain lion and hoofprints of deer are wound in graceful filigree.

What leaf-fringed legend haunts about thy shape? asked Keats of the urn as we could of these tracks by the river. Is this the record of two animals that passed at separate times, sharing the canyon's life-blood? Or is this evidence of mortal chase, a frozen moment before deer's narrow survival or lion's successful kill?

The figures of poised animation that haunted Keats were lovers and village celebrants, not predator and prey. Yet beneath the sweetness of tone and stateliness of language lies a similar motif. *What mad pursuit? What struggle to escape?* The figures suggest men or gods in pursuit of *maidens loth,* and a lover *winning near the goal,* presumably over opposition. The moment of capture may be as pleasurable to the vanquished as to the victor, but its accomplishment involves the flight of female from male, of mortal from deity, in the vocabulary of stalker and prey.

Finding that victory in love's chase leads to emotional death, *A burning forehead, and a parching tongue,* Keats turns to the lovers' village pursuing its own larger celebration. *Who are these coming to the sacrifice? To what green altar, O mysterious priest, Lead'st thou that heifer lowing at the skies?* The villagers are commemorating death itself, giving it ritual significance precisely with the death of an animal. Their social, physical death formalizes private and emotional death. Are they enacting mortality to subdue it? Are they trying to reconcile dying to the communal mind? Keats leaves us alone with the evidence: love pursued to the taste of ashes, society responding to death with ceremony.

The questions posed by the figures on the urn and the tracks in Escalante sand are convergent: what is the nature of a world that proceeds by hunter and quarry, by triumph indissoluble from death? For Keats, writing in 1819 during the first wave of Romanticism, the terms of combat were new and less clearly defined. But already the celestial clockwork of the preceding century was giving way to a concept of life as competition and struggle. Coleridge was lecturing on evolution, and forty years later Darwin was to provide the mechanism by which it operates. Society became the struggle of individuals, the developing economy was industrial capitalism, and Delacroix was painting sulphurous canvases of lions attacking deer.

Our own vision a century and a half later, in the form of environmentalism, is largely an elaboration of that same vision. The recent sciences of ethology and ecology are showing us the principles of animal behavior and the process of interwoven life communities, while genetics and agricultural manipulation show us how to bend those principles to our presumed advantage. The great chain of being turns out to be a food chain, a pyramid of increasing predation of which humanity is the apex. And as Americans at the apex of human well-being, we preside over cattle shot full of hormones in the stupefaction of feedlots, and poultry multiplied in fluorescent catacombs: sentient life turned out on the assembly line. With feeling increasingly suspected in plants, even the vegetarian dodge looks unlike moral salvation. Our new knowledge, deflecting the biosphere toward our dinner table, has cost us our innocence about the predatory basis of earthly life. Yet all the latest disciplines and technologies have provided no answers; they have merely sharpened the questions. We are stuck with the motif of the chase: lover pursuing beloved, civilization engaged in ritual sacrifice, lion pursuing deer, mankind swallowing the earth. Stare at the trampled sand. *Thou silent form dost tease us out of thought/ As does eternity.*

Cold pastoral! exclaims Keats, temporarily blanking at what has become too vast to encompass—and then proceeds to his resolution. And what he offers us is not explanation but extracted pattern, not celebrants and lovers but time frozen for inspection and revealing the shape of our lives. It is the hunt at its most telling moment: lovers on the brink of consummation, procession before ritual sacrifice. What survives of those moments is not participant but witness, not lovers and villages but their tracks in the sand: an urn. Individuals will come and go, as they have in the more than two millennia between the firing of the urn and the composition of the ode, and the century and a half between the ode and this year's tracks by the Escalante River—to which we add our own. The urn, because it makes satisfying pattern out of passing feelings, is beautiful, and because it is the structure of our lives, it is true. And indecipherable marks of pursuit and flight are true for us still. What must survive as friend to man, in silent testimonial, are stained rock, running stream, willow and cattail and rabbit brush, and a ribbon of sand with its decorative frieze of lion and deer. It is not for us to understand them; only to count on them.

Slickrock and the Bach Chaconne

Bruce
Berger

Amateur pianists, obsessive as a breed, are impossible about their hands. When the temperature drops below forty I conjure frostbite, and recall too often that time I rammed a scorpion with a thesaurus in a Phoenix kitchen and bent my little finger the wrong way. There are moments when the desert, my other obsession, seems to aim every dagger at my clumsy, aspiring technique. And the desert, true to character, landed its blow when I was least on guard.

A friend had stopped to rinse a gravel-choked sneaker in a small pool. I sluffed my pack against a tree and settled on the only perch, a pointed knob of sandstone. I leaned back on one hand to take the rest of my weight, watched my friend dutifully rinse the sock, turn it right side out, wring it, pull it on, cram a wet foot into a wet sneaker, pull the lace, form the bow . . . Suddenly the rock sheered in the middle, and eight inches of sandstone, capped with my bulk, landed on the fourth digit of my right hand.

The nail was instantly black. A bit of blood jetted from the tip, and skin was scraped from the second joint. I felt for broken bones, detected none, and found the rest of my hand unscathed. The finger was less painful than icy and numb; I held it like a cracked fetish as we rushed back up the canyon to camp. There was no remedy but to wash it thoroughly, wrap a bandaid around the fingertip, and take a belt of 151 proof rum for perspective.

Because the injury was to my right hand rather than my left, the incident oddly meshed with a more blissful event on a previous canyon trip. Our party included a concert violinist from New York who needed to keep in practice for an upcoming recital. Lashed to his pack was a fiddle whose maker had told him, "It's one of my rejects. Take it to the desert, tell me what it does, and don't worry." Daily we heard a warm-up of scales and figures coming from his hiding place. On the night of the full moon we gathered on a sandstone shelf, someone produced a candle melted into a manhattan glass, and our friend unfurled the Bach *Chaconne*. The only other sound was the slur of moving water.

Cold light emptied into the canyon, turning one wall a luminous pocked silver, leaving the other a hulking darkness stopped by a line that inched toward us as the music progressed. I had heard the *Chaconne* before, with half-attention and most often in orchestral arrangements, and felt I was hearing another piece. As the violin worked through the minor variations, the listeners emerged one by one in the moonlight. We were covered with radiance by the time the music broke into the major. When the piece returned to the dark opening chords, it was impossible not to be struck by the vastness of the architecture, laboring intensely toward peace, celebration, and back to severity. Almost all organized sound seems to profane the desert, or any great landscape. But the *Chaconne*, with its massive journey from austerity to tenderness and back— as if through rock and water—seemed to concur in shape with the very walls that echoed its passage.

The *Chaconne* is the last movement of Bach's *Partita No. 2 in D minor for violin unaccompanied,* opens from a complete partita like the tail of a peacock, and has lived the career of a free-floating monument. Among the transcriptions for assorted instruments is one for piano by Busoni, with two recordings currently in catalogue, and a more obscure arrangement by Brahms for the left hand alone. Contrived in 1879 as an exercise to develop the dexterity of the left hand, or perhaps as a musical folly, it sat at the back of my *Brahms Klavier-Werke, Band II*, as a kind of consolation prize if my right hand were ever knocked out of commission. It was, ironically, a canyon in Utah that first revealed to me the immensity of the Bach *Chaconne*, and a canyon three drainages away that sent me in desperation to the score.

On previous occasions I had lost toenails, watched them grow back in a month, and assumed I had a month to get a grip on the *Chaconne*. I kept the loose fingernail of the right hand bandaged, lest I snag it off before the replacement was ready, and plugged away at Bach-Brahms. As the new nail took shape in the dark, the opening variations, more pocked than luminous, grew under the strengthening left hand. Take the bandage off and let it breathe, said a medically knowledgeable friend. When the bandage did slip off in the shower, there was my dead nail, now ghostly white, arched over something mysterious. The skin around it was unattractive; better to keep the whole thing under wraps until the job was done. I worked my way to the lush, delicious major. The old nail was looser; I peeked through the end and glimpsed a kind of grey mush. So one hand was semi-composing, the other decomposing . . . I reached the return of the minor. The old nail was half a flange but I didn't dare pry it too far, even for inspection. It was three months since I had sat on the defective rock, and the *Chaconne* was shakily memorized. For God's sake let your skin breathe! insisted my knowledgeable friend. When the bandage slid off in the next shower, it took the nail with it. Revealed was the lower half of a new fingernail, looking normal, while the rest was a kind of puckered thickening I was afraid even to touch.

"Is this *normal* for a new fingernail?" I asked my friend. "After all these months, is this all I get?"

"Normal for a pianist. You'd probably have trouble growing toenails if you were a dancer. Look, nails are an evolutionary vestige. They're claws on the way out. If it

Bruce Berger

doesn't grow back all the way, you'll get tough skin that will do just as well."

In another month my right fourth finger sported a smooth polished nail, indistinguishable from the rest. The *Chaconne* too was smooth, needing the deepening only time can provide, and meanwhile my left hand, as Brahms intended, was a newly adequate partner to my right. The canyons that led on the one hand to a new nail, and on the other hand to Bach, took millennia to cut to their present depth—but the geological span is a luxury we lack. Time is uneven, unfair, and lands unpredictable blows. It is also the only medium. Whether we're canyons or musicians, we must dig into it and shape what we can.

The
Telling
Distance

Science, Environmentalism, and Music

Bruce
Berger

It has never been adequately explained why environmentalists and research scientists tend to an interest in
music, particularly classical music, wildly surpassing probability. Physicists at universities and laboratories across the
country regularly meet to read through scores and give
chamber recitals. *Not Man Apart*, the publication of
Friends of the Earth, has noted with awe the number of
environmentalists who are part-time musicians. Many
immersed in abstract theory relax by playing with the local
symphony, or by listening to extensive record collections,
and almost emblematic is the figure of Einstein, who
insisted on playing, however badly, the violin. A certain
correlation would be anticipated because of educational
levels and the cultural matrix, but why music in particular,
in such percentages, with such fanaticism?

Music seems to inhabit the mercurial dark at the human
center, and the ability of patterned sound to become
charged with our feeling is an enigma that still ends, like
music itself, in silence. For kinds of music that appeal to the
brain as well as the bone to be pleasurable to certain kinds
of people is less mysterious. Some hidden bond must link
the scientist and the environmentalist with the musician—
a bond which I believe to be their common rage for
systems.

Consider the infant just learning to walk. His humanity
is already absorbed in the process of distinguishing self
from nonself, and sorting the nonself into dog, chair,

Mama, food, caca. At the same time he is abstracting those externals into some interior system of words. If Noam Chomsky is right, words themselves, regardless of culture, await a built-in syntax, some master language within which all languages fall. Just as the seed is coded with the plant, the human brain is ripe with the patterns that will bloom into the human complexity. We are from birth spinners of systems.

Systemizing proceeds through stages. Between first grammar and adolescence comes the acquisitive stage, one which many of us never leave. It is the dread age of collecting: rocks, coins, stamps, model planes, baseball cards. As adults we may substitute antiques, African violets or pornography, but the unstated goal is still the same: when the collection is complete one has *all* of one's chosen category. Life in its extravagance is too vast for possession, but the collector can isolate some element small enough for purchase. Any collection expanding toward its goal of completeness gives the satisfaction of an acquired language, a new system.

With adolescence and adulthood come new levels of abstraction. Now it is perhaps a passion for maps, for visiting all the National Parks or Wilderness Areas, for reading all of one author, for photographing the high-lights of one's travels or one's life, for amassing friends, money, votes, sexual conquests. Systems become less an array of objects than a rainbow of memories and achieve-ments intended to give pleasure across the spectrum. That it does not is irrelevant; the joy is to proceed.

At the highest system-gathering short of mystical fu-sion, the mind seeks to understand the relation of each component to its fellows so as to grasp how a system adapts, evolves and survives as a breathing creature. At this point one turns into an economist, an astronomer, a biologist, a physicist, a student of politics, anthropology, ecosystems, medicine or the law. With sufficient brass one becomes an expert. In mankind's eyes, and particularly one's own, one has reached an enviable plateau; one has captured a system alive.

To fuse our amateur musicians, the abstract scientist and the environmentalist, consider what the brain faces trying to absorb a single ecosystem. It begins over like a child, isolating and naming the parts: microbes, insects, plants, mammals, the airborne and the aquatic, all animal and vegetable organisms and everything in between. Next the burden of assembly: how does it relate to its context in the mineral world? What are the food chains? How does it divide up territory? How does it adapt to changes in climate, sudden gaps in the food chain, blooms and eclipses of species, the rise of one form and decline of another? What, indeed *are* the variables? Most fiendishly, how does it perceive itself? One must consider that many organisms are blind, react only to variations in temperature, see only in two dimensions or in shades of grey, possess hearing or scent or sight keener than our own, or have senses like sonar which we lack entirely. No creature may be aware that other creatures perceive it at all, yet their exclusive realities meld into a fabric with its own dynamics of organization, change, and endurance—a super-organism that sustains itself perhaps blindly, but correctly. Aldo Leopold enjoined his fellow forest rangers, before they meddled with their territories, to "think like a mountain." Good but impossible advice: with perception splintered into as many modes as there are species, only God, if he so chose, could think like a mountain. It seems clear that anyone who tackles one of the abstract sciences feels impelled to take systemizing to the limit. The task is necessarily hopeless, for the physicist as well as the ecologist. The variables themselves are too numerous to be identified. Our knowledge of them comes through five senses as arbitrary and isolated as those of any other creature, or from the sense-extending machines that have blossomed since the Renaissance. For the student of ecology the task involves sensibilities that

Bruce Berger

are alien and inaccessible, and for the physicist a range from the infinitesimal to the cosmic that baffles the human scale. There is the further limitation of our imagination, well expressed by the physicist who said that "the universe is not only queerer than we suppose, but queerer than we can suppose." The apprehension of any transhuman system is a mirage that flees geometrically as one approaches.

Complete knowledge of a system, then, can only be possible under one condition—that it be wholly human in origin. Yet many such systems exist. Spun by the human imagination out of the shapes, colors, sounds, solids, and spaces of this world, out of the languages of word, number, and tone, and out of our sense of proportion, they are the arts. Unless experimentally computed for randomness, art depends upon choice, deliberate or unconscious, of the human brain upon materials to hand. Each category of art, within the limitations of its medium and its rules to be followed or broken, is its own system, accessible because it is secreted out of ourselves.

And of all the arts, music is the most transparent to pure form. Upon our emotions it is the most direct. At times it almost demands that we move in time, be carried along, ride its melodic crests and step to its rhythms. It will not let go of our memories. Yet even as music insists through our blood it permits us to wield our intelligence upon its relation of parts, its symmetries and oppositions, its unfolding balance. To thread the labyrinth any composer sets off produces a mental exhilaration that runs parallel to, but is distinct from, the raw sweep of emotion.

The composer is the quintessential creator of systems. It is his province to produce the most perfect, or the grandest, or the most exquisitely chiseled construct of which he is capable, whether song, sonata or symphony. He may not rationally understand how a certain passage came to be, just as artists in all fields have attested to the sensation of creation simply coming *through* them, but the greater the composer, the more mysterious the ease with which he will satisfy and still surprise—and the greater the challenge to the listener. "Music is feeling, then, not sound," says Wallace Stevens; "You are the music while the music lasts," says T. S. Eliot. Music allows you to *be* a system even as you trace its whorls and reversals.

Like the child, like the ecologist, the listener begins in ignorance, a strand at a time: the notes of a phrase, the phrases of a melody, the overlapping of melodies, the harmonies that engender further elaborations—music's atoms and galaxies, its spiraling energy, its explosions, its mass and empty space, its organizing gravity. The viola in a quartet, a horn passage in a symphony, a recurrent or fleeting motif, a strand of polyphony among many—in the community of systems these are the dolphins that leap through the current, the keening of the hawk, the nibblers among roots and the great winged migrations. Struggling for dominance, harmonizing in symbiosis, working its destiny in baroque stasis, in romantic evolution or in contemporary leaps and gaps—each factor unraveling as if unaware of its place in the composite—music is the career of a complete organism, its adaptations, its disappearances, its summits, and its final silence. Yet music is also the product of a single human brain, and offers the listener a single statement. Perhaps what is so satisfying to the physicist, the astronomer, the outdoor enthusiast, the seeker of wholes—and the final seduction of music—is this: music is not a system of objects, but a paradigm of systems. It satisfies the cerebral hunger even as it engages our deepest feelings.

Music as a metaphor for existence, of course, is no novelty. Pythagoras took it quite literally, and when he found that the division of vibrating strings by whole numbers created the sounds most harmonious to the ear, believed he had decoded creation's own harmony. The Ptolemaic system sang those harmonies with crystal spheres. Myths in which Orpheus creates harmony out of chaos

Bruce Berger

parallel the division of light from darkness, the firmament from the waters, in a kind of musical Genesis.

The musical universe did not die with Copernicus. In this century Rilke has based his personal mysticism on Orphic myths and Eliot has shaped his in musical form with the *Four Quartets*. The composer Scriabin believed he discovered a musical symmetry in the bisected octave—the augmented fourth or flatted fifth—and his converts have attested to experiencing through his music a blinding white light and other transcendent phenomena. Claude Levi-Strauss, whose *Le Cru et le Cuit* is based like the Eliot poems on musical forms, has said that to think mythologically is to think musically. There are books expounding *The Symphony of Life*, and the possibilities of metaphoric degeneration are as available as bad music itself. But most significantly for us there is contemporary physics with its great cosmic and subatomic patterns, its evolving symmetries of quarks and neutrinos, the double helix of molecular biology, all the spiraling configurations of matter which is, as it turns out, interchangeable with energy. The universe, says Sir James Jeans, begins to resemble a gigantic thought—and, one might almost add, a musical thought.

But it is a thought most of us will never think. Hiking the ecosystem with cameras and guide books, listening to recordings, shuffling through chaos with our five thin senses, most of us feel clever enough just to find the trail. We look up and promptly forget the names of our fellow coordinates until the next time they bloom or sting us or fly past. We listen to Brahms, relishing but not quite grasping how a passage, satisfactory in passing, answers to the whole. But once in a while our binoculars catch an oriole braiding its nest out of a fan palm, or hear in the second theme a slow inversion of the first. Those insights tell us little more than the data they connect, but they offer just the exhilaration, the sense of penetration, which is joy in the mind.

To reproduce the universe inside, in imitation of our gods, is our upward mobility. Human intelligence, divine theft that it is, is still isolated and frail, its patterns only tentative. But those systems are vital to consciousness as we know it, and as the only species so obsessed, we are the music while the music lasts.

Bruce Berger

THE USES

OF EMPTINESS

Much Ado about Nothing

Everything in the arroyo flees from your footsteps. Lizards scatter into the nearest cracked rock. Quail hover in shadow, hoping you'll take them for stones, and at the last moment they burst into birds. Snakes evaporate, doves squeak skyward, rabbits crazyleg at a dead heat. As for fox, mountain lion and coyote, they melt into legend, leaving only their tracks and their scat. The arroyo, channeling what there is of water, luring you on toward life that vanishes, is the very heart of the desert. And the heart of the arroyo, the desert's heart of hearts, is pale evacuated sand.

It is another emptiness that launches your eye from a vantage point, sails it over a desert valley swirling with arroyos, gashed perhaps with canyons, and impales it—like a shrike with its prey—on a spiked horizon. This is not the calm of infinity but a precise, carved absence, full of hard objects, guiding you outward until vision pulls taut. Bound with such surreal articulation, this is the barrenness that draws imagination to its edge.

But the most telling emptiness lies between living things. For the desert plant, exiled by thirst, catching water with its roots, exposed on all sides, in competition with its own kind, emptiness is the very source of life. Desert adaptation may be no more remarkable than that of the forest, the jungle, the prairie or the sea, but it exposes life for what it is: conjured out of nothing. Here, from the nothing of drought, the nothing of life in flight, the nothing of sheer space, we miraculously are.

We might well ask, what is the use of such places? To the usual replies—they are consoling, they add to the planet's diversity, we have to put bombing ranges *somewhere*—we might add the more recent answers along U. S. 80 between Socorro, New Mexico, and Springerville, Arizona.

One example shows for miles in the distance, filling the immense Plains of San Agustin with what looks like a piece of contextual art depicting desert primroses. This ancient lakebed was chosen from forty candidates because it had the least interference from radio and television transmitters, least disturbance from vehicles and aircraft, had a southerly view of the heavens, and suggested a vast ear open to the sky. The primroses are the twenty-seven radio dishes of the Very Large Array, a radio telescope tuned to the longest vibrations of the electromagnetic spectrum. *Bruce Berger* Each dish is eighty-two feet across, attached to a Y-shaped railroad track whose legs are twenty kilometers long, allowing the dishes to be grouped in different configurations. At their farthest extension they fall short of filling the valley.

Surrounded by the sherds of Folsom Man, the oldest of our kind to inhabit the continent, these antennae chart the radio emissions of visible galaxies, pulsars, and non-visible radio galaxies whose cores may be black holes. They also pick up the farthest, fastest receding—and therefore the oldest—objects in the universe itself, quasars that pack the energy of galaxies into the circumference of stars. Under these white sensors, when vehicles on U. S. 80 fall silent, one hears the gurgling of meadowlarks, then a silence in which the whole valley seems to be listening in. A finite emptiness, impressive in earthly terms, has been rigged to receive information from the limits of time and space.

At Quemado, New Mexico, fifty-five miles west of the Very Large Array, one can arrange to be driven an hour north to an actual piece of contextual art known as The Lightning Field. Four hundred stainless steel poles stand in a precise grid, one mile by one kilometer, so impeccably planted that their points would evenly support an imaginary cookie sheet. In another of New Mexico's grand valleys, bounded by blue ranges and heaped by weather, the metal spikes seem lost. Compared with the flowerlike Very Large Array they look like a schematic tree farm, nor are they allowed to tilt at the two gracefully creaking windmills nearby. The woman who drives visitors to the site has watched many storms without seeing lightning strike a pole, and believes lightning actually avoids them. She has concluded that the field is intended as a *tribute* to lightning, and as for her neighbors, art for them is "still pictures and statues."

The California-based creator, Walter de Maria, lived in New York for seventeen years before completing The Lightning Field, and previously designed a work in which mile-long bulldozer cuts in the deserts of three continents would be superimposed by aerial photograph for viewing in a gallery. For this earth sculptor The Lightning Field probably represents a breakthrough in sensitivity, but the visitor—who is not permitted to experience The Lightning Field for less than twenty-four hours—may become more absorbed in the horned toads, the less pedantic points of the sawtooth mountains, the gunmetal dust exposed by the teeth of cattle. Still, twenty-five employees worked on site for five months, thirty-two companies participated, and all of it was paid for by foundations and private benefactors for whom this particular use of emptiness must have filled an emotional gap.

Whatever one thinks of either of these new uses of the desert, they were completed within three years of each other only a short while back, and represent the recent avant-garde in science and art. These inventions are appearing at a moment when we are discovering the literal emptiness of the universe and of ourselves. The atoms of all matter, including those of our flesh, measure one hundred millionth of an inch across, and blown up to the

The Telling Distance

size of sports arenas their nuclei would still be no more than grains of sand. So widely spaced are those grains that subatomic particles called neutrinos, raining continuously through the universe, can pass through this packed earth without encountering a lonely atom, as if we weren't here. Solid matter, at its elementary level, eludes isolation at all, and only *tends* to exist—as event, as statistical probability, as sheer relationship. The smaller the scale, the vaster the apparent emptiness. Physicist Heinz Pagels, in *Perfect Symmetry,* notes that there is a gap, representing thirteen powers of ten, between the particles called W and Z gluons and the still smaller X gluons. He calls this gap a microworld "desert" and in his chart he populates it with saguaros.

Corner electrons and they panic like lizards. Pinpoint infinity and space curves back on itself like a New Mexican valley. Locate the emptiness of the flesh, or of the self, and isolation turns to self-knowledge. Contemporary physics, having passed through mechanism, has arrived at numerical odds, dissolving events, tissues of relationships, "virtual" particles whose virtue lies in their resistance to detection. Such revelations lie beyond reach of us obtuse, non-hypothetical laymen caught in our five solid, stone-kicking senses. But the desert is being geared to probe the emptiness of the outer limits and of the self. Gazing across it until it becomes a vast analog, a sermon in sand, cosmic emptiness seems almost close enough to touch.

Bruce Berger

Time Out

To blend one's consciousness with the universe seems pretentious to a Westerner and to strive for ego loss seems a contradiction in terms—but I was briefly tricked into something like it late one afternoon, driving through Monument Valley. The stranded formations were deep-shadowed, russet and cayenne in the low sun. A few horses wandered in scrawny solitude and each sage seemed lit an independent silver-green. I was enjoying it all in a touristic way, in that last light that flares each object with its own radiance, and particularly I relished the shadow of my own jeep passing over the sage like an elongated Model T. To be the eccentric eye through all that deepened color was personally satisfying. Suddenly the jeep passed into the shadow of a monument, the image I so identified with vanished, and the rest of my awareness was sprung loose. For an instant I felt, this is how the place would feel without an external intelligence: landscape *aware of itself.* My thought spread out for a moment, freed from its source; then I caught myself being aware of my own absence, identity flooded back, and long before the jeep emerged from shadow my brain was back in my skull.

The
Telling
Distance

Borges Primitive Area

Bruce
Berger

S een from above it is quite finite: eighty or one hundred
square miles of white Cedar Mesa sandstone set in the
more monolithic crimson formations, a pale inlay in a red
horizon, a catacomb open to the sky. Even hiking its
northern boundary along the wash which drains it, you
would find only layers of bright rock, spangling cottonwoods, the spires and seeps routine for this remarkable
land. It is when you start south from the main drainage,
burrowing into pure stone, that another prospect emerges.
The principal cuts twist and fray into numberless side
canyons, which similarly twist and fray, so that one unwit-
tingly wanders onward, hypnotized that the system has no
determined end. It becomes implausible that so many
snaking and interlocking canyons could fit into a land so
precisely circumscribed: as if stone were mirror refracting
each corridor into further potential, falsifying perspective
until one's skin ceased to be a point of reference. Tracing
your footsteps back through the sand to the friends you
casually left, you would half expect them to have turned
into strangers.

In an open labyrinth, what beast? Find a high cave and
wait, for the creature is visible but has no shape. Massing
out of the sky, collecting in the mesas, fusing with unpredictable fury in the canyons which twist and repeat and
fray, the minotaur is water. Its formless rush upon dumb
stone creates shape in the way that generation upon
generation of developing thought, on a more Lamarckian
planet, might have carved the human brain. Materializing

from the air, disappearing into the ground or escaping back into the sky to be born over and over again, the beast creates and destroys its own labyrinth. But the cycle's end in time, as well as in space, will elude a brain long gone from its cave.

The
Telling
Distance

The Stone Gallery

Slickrock that leaps unexpectedly into a dome, an arch, a spire, causes a similar leap in the hiker's pulse. Stone and erosion, working their uniform processes, seem newly charged with the miraculous, and the dullest sandstone is suddenly potent with twists and acrobatics on its journey back to sand. One learns again that unexpectedness is the wellspring of beauty.

But name the phenomenon Druid Arch, Yellowstone Falls, Zabriskie Point, Capitol Lake or Devil's Tower, and put it in Arches National Park, Death Valley National Monument or the Maroon-Snowmass Wilderness Area. Suddenly the object detaches itself from its context, gains an invisible frame and becomes a classic. Gone is the weave of intricate forces; one senses instead the hand of the individual. The tide of nature is parted for the revelation of some miracle, and behind the miracle is the Word with its single, limiting vision. For reasons lost in the matrix of language, the christening of a piece of nature transforms it into a work of art.

Our national parks and monuments, promising continuity, respite and pre-civilized experience, have increasingly become mazes of human language. One goes there to regain some nameless belonging, only to encounter a catalogued gallery. Displays at park headquarters instruct one in proper appreciation. Roads, trails and signs lead from one novelty to another. And the scenic loops are studded with statuesque wonders, set landscapes and

Bruce Berger

panoramic climaxes. Yellowstone is a British Museum of natural anomalies. The Tetons are composed as The Last Supper. The Grand Canyon is water's consummate sculpture. Our parks provide essentially a ceremonial experience, through which an informed public passes properly awed, and exiled from its own feelings.

Park custodians have the same weakness as the rest of us: they love to name, to isolate, to point out and to enshrine. A friend and I once hiked in Capitol Reef toward some formation whose provocative title I have forgotten. Stenciled footprints like a yellow zipper drew us across the bedrock. The right foot was twice as large as the left, and at first we had a fine time imagining this lopsided pedant so typical of park planners. The rest of the slickrock, the junipers, the lichen, the hard earth and blue sky were brilliantly anonymous as ever. But those yellow footprints, marching us toward some scenic aberration, deadened us to the routine loveliness of where we were. The zipper was in poor taste, but it was the failure of our own sensibilities to keep it in scale. Realizing that our goal could only be the climactic letdown, we returned to the parking lot and fled to less ceremonial terrain beyond the park.

It is too bad that things arrowed and tagged lose their vitality. The industrial web is closing in, and never had we more need of the nameless. All American land now lies in some public or private category, but that is not enough. It seems we can only save our last wilderness by culling it from its random occurrence in National Forest and BLM lands, and transferring it to the sharper boundaries and stricter confinements of legislated Wilderness. We can only rescue what's wild by expanding the process of Babel.

It is our twist to an old paradox: that our rage for order craves the very structure our thirst for adventure flees. As technology gathers control, our fences are both tighter and more invisible, our internal map more strung with secret barbed wire. And perhaps the most diehard adventurers, who avoid designated wilderness as fiercely as they avoid parks and monuments, are those in most desperate flight from the plats, grids, and ghostly projections of our own brains.

Bruce
Berger

Art Deco Mirage

Twin bald eagles of cement, ten feet high, ride like mastheads over the Gila River. In shadow at their feet stand three egg-shaped domes, each over 200 feet high. Spillways, flaring toward the canyon walls and converging at the riverbed, compose the huge sculpture in a heart-shaped frame. Coolidge Dam, on the San Carlos Apache Reservation in southeastern Arizona, is further proof that the surrealist painters were correct to stage their strange particulars in the desert.

First conceived in 1896, Coolidge Dam traveled a strange path in becoming reclamation's tribute to art deco. The site, where the Gila River veers west from the San Carlos Valley, to enter a tight canyon that conducts it through the Mescal Mountains to the dry plains of central Arizona, is of a sort to make an engineer dream of contracts. Encouraged by passage of the National Reclamation Act in 1902, delayed by World War I, the project finally passed Congress with $5.5 million in appropriations in 1924. That was the era of messianic reclamation, when dams were to replace six-shooters in advancing civilization, and water engineering was almost a romantic profession. Coolidge Dam was singled out to be a showpiece. It would incorporate the new engineering principles, it would generate excitement for further water projects, and it would be a work of art.

The actual design is the result of three years of calculation by Major Charles Olberg, of the U. S. Indian Service. It was to be the world's first large-scale multiple dome dam, consisting of three parallel egg-shaped domes whose hollows faced downstream. The structure would be supported by two massive piers, flanking the central dome, and anchored at the sides to the canyon walls. Use of steel reinforcements within the concrete would eliminate the need for the usual joints that allow for expansion and contraction. The dome walls, tapering from twenty-one feet at the base to four feet at the top, were engineered to conduct the shear forces to the buttresses as the domes reached their crest. With its facade of three hollows, the dam would reproduce in concrete what nature perfected in the eggshell.

Construction, using largely Apache labor, began on January 1, 1927. Under supervision of the U. S. Indian Service, a division of the Department of Interior, a crushing, washing and screening plant for the aggregate was installed on the streambed a mile below the dam, using material near the site itself. The aggregate rode to the mixing plant by aerial tramway, eliminating the need for trucks to contend with a flooding river, and the concrete was cast into panels that could be used practically without change in shape throughout the domes. Because of its vaulted structure, each tier was self-supporting and the dam was raised without scaffolding. When the structure stood complete, all surfaces, including the interior of the domes, were finished with a surface compound that smoothed the exterior, and the decorative features were added last. The dam was dedicated on March 4, 1930, near the end of Prohibition and the beginning of the Depression. Before a crowd of 15,000 Anglos, with a scattering of Indians and a few of mixed blood like Will Rogers, ex-President Coolidge delivered one of his least reticent speeches, then smashed a bottle of water against a bronze plaque.

But dams are not mere sculptures; they are agents of change. Behind Coolidge Dam lay the town of San Carlos, an Indian agency and headquarters of the San

Bruce Berger

Carlos Indian Reservation. Founded in 1872 by agreement with the newly subdued Apaches, San Carlos lay in a valley where Apache chieftains once roamed, and where Geronimo was brought back to jail. By the time of the filling of the reservoir, some 550 Indians living in one hundred homes and wickiups had to be relocated to a new town ten miles away. Traders, missionaries and government agents salvaged what they could, and buildings too sturdy to be moved were dynamited. Twenty miles of track belonging to the Southern Pacific Railroad were realigned at a cost of $2.4 million, with the government paying the first million. The greatest problem turned out to be the Apache burial ground, for the Indians refused to allow the bones of their ancestors to be disturbed by relocation or invaded by water. A compromise was struck whereby a large slab of concrete projecting four feet downward on each side was laid over the cemetery, presumably sealing the dead.

It was the Apaches who lost their town and river valley, and their ancient enemies, the more settled and agrarian Pimas, who received the irrigation. Downstream, beginning seventy-five miles west of the dam, the Gila River was ladled out through canals and diversion dams to an area once irrigated on a more modest scale by the ancient Hohokam. Of the 100,000 acres reached by the water, half was owned by Anglo settlers and half by the Pimas, making Coolidge Dam the first major reclamation project largely intended to benefit Native Americans. Crops have included citrus, alfalfa, lettuce, melons and dates. But the principal growth, it turns out, has been cotton, a surplus crop that requires vast amounts of water, leaves the soil depleted, and whose market for Arizonans is now mainly Asian. Water from the dam has enabled both Anglos and Indians to support themselves for a time through agriculture, but when the farmland is exhausted, the dam's net effect may prove to be ruinous. This makeshift agricultural area, meanwhile, has given birth to a new town named, uncoincidentally, Coolidge.

Today's visitor may find Coolidge Dam as obscure as its consequences. The road leads off U. S. 70 between Globe and Safford, and skirts the edge of the reservoir, to arrive at an odd pair of cement pillars. Walkways with intricate railings line the road on either side, offering glimpses of an immense dropoff to the west. So like an esplanade is the dam's rim that the most wheelbound motorist may park for a stroll.

The pedestrian is first stopped by the square pillars, busy with ionic pilasters, a protrusion like a sculpted treble clef, a formal cornice, and a crowning metal and glass beacon whose eight projecting torches bear eight empty light sockets. Stepping onto the walkway, one follows a railing set with scrolls and blossoms on rhythmic panels. On the upstream side the surrounding mountains hang in the reservoir's pastels, while the tops of the three domes, colonized by moss, bulge eerily underfoot. Between the domes, projecting over the dam's two buttresses, are twin piers leading to hexagonal platforms that seem to cry for band gazebos and summer dances.

On the downstream side one is struck first by the gorge itself, with its buff limestone strata tilted downstream so that they seem to converge on the water, while saguaros and chaparral cling to the canyon walls. Stepping onto the eagle-bearing projections one can look down on the eagles themselves, the farther sculpture in fierce profile, the one immediately below silhouetted against the greenish swirl from the penstocks. At close range one can admire the intricate carving of the neck feathers, the beaks whitened by birds that may not be eagles, the cracks in the cement. Unrealized was that an aggregate that expanded when wet was included in the ornaments, gradually splitting them, and only dry air has preserved what would have crumbled in a more saturated climate.

But the full drama will be missed if one neglects the dirt road that switchbacks from the north wall of the canyon to

Bruce Berger

the bottom. Not for the acrophobic, it can be driven if you don't mind a tight passage with an oncoming car; better still, it can be walked. Only from downstream does the full symmetry of the dam come into perspective, with its deep-shadowed vaults, and the railing that doubles as a cornice. Obtrusive in this most artistic of dams is a small power plant at the dam's base, shooting water through its two penstocks and launching electricity on powerlines to a tower on the canyon's north rim, from which it disappears over the Mescal Mountains toward Hayden. The dam was built purely for irrigation, but a hydroelectric plant was later added to defray expenses. The plant has sunk because of a weak substratum, and the water users being billed for a new plant are suing. Serene above all this pettiness, on tulip-shaped swellings between the domes, stand the eagles. Feet planted wide, wings stretched out like human arms, or like vultures sunning their wings for the day's first flight—but not like eagles— they gaze toward something unseen in the sky. The irony they are fixed on, one feels sure, is the brilliant future of reclamation.

Behind the eagles and their dam lies San Carlos Lake, literally a winding sheet of water over the old town of San Carlos. Twenty-five miles long and three miles across at its widest point, San Carlos Lake is one of those shapeless reservoirs that fills a flat alluvial valley, reflecting the scenery decently when full and puckering into mudflats at the least drawdown, leaving its shore in geographical limbo. A number of times San Carlos Lake has dried completely, allowing former residents and the historically-minded to walk the old townsite and poke at the foundations of the trading post, the Lutheran mission, the jail. Like all reservoirs in Arizona, San Carlos is recreational, with marinas and services maintained by the San Carlos Apaches, and it is duly patronized by Arizonans, who own more boats per capita than residents of any other state. But it is not high on their list.

It may be the disenchantment of the reservoir, and the fact that the dam hides its full facade from most visitors, that has kept Coolidge Dam in obscurity ever since its glamorous dedication. A rare period piece, as an icon it expresses a faith in reclamation that only a few contractors still hold onto. Unglimpsed was our age of massive cost overruns, overstrained budgets, a decreasing willingness to lose what remains of river habitat, and a deadend in which, from an engineering standpoint, the best damsites are already supplied with dams. Where the eagles look to a cornucopian future, we look back on fifty years of that future and find ambiguity. It is unlikely we will see heroic new wedges of concrete, and we will certainly not see them sculpted.

If Coolidge Dam has added meaning, it has lost nothing as spectacle. It is listed on the National Register of Historic Places, and as a piece of functional masonry it is far more interesting than the overvisited London Bridge, on the other side of Arizona. A mirage in concrete, Coolidge Dam makes a worthy pilgrimage for anyone who wants to sense the millennial fervor that even bureaucrats once felt toward salvation through water. Not soon again will our republic express itself in a work so eccentric, so enthusiastic, so naive.

Bruce Berger

Back Country

The junipers and piñons that held the road tight, thick and evenly spaced in the red earth, suddenly opened to a thirty-acre gap of trees indiscriminately heaped, splintered, mangled, shriveled, strewn on the ground, their needles brown, their trunks a mass of raw breaks, as if an entire forest had died of nerve gas. We pulled off and got out. On foot the devastation was still more wrenching. We picked our way obscurely through the woody litter, over scarred topsoil with plumes of dust in our nostrils, over and around aggregations of limbs where twists of surveyor's tape glittered like scraps of neon.

So this was chaining, that process whereby the Forest Service and the Bureau of Land Management tighten a heavy chain between two bulldozers that move parallel through a stand of small trees, knocking over all that intervenes, even junipers up to a thousand years old. Opening up new meadows for the deer to browse, claimed the agencies. Enabling the state to sell more hunting licenses, we concluded bitterly, or still more likely, creating more pasturage for local ranchers with grazing allotments on public lands.

We toured the ruins, crawling over downed timber and nicking our skin, thinking evil thoughts about our tax dollars, when a dark triangle like a primeval bird shot overhead, followed by a crack of sound that shook the earth and our very spines, then a protracted scream. The creature was followed by another and another, a whole flight of bombers that seemed barely a hundred feet

The Telling Distance

213

overhead, courtesy, we assumed, of the Air Force Academy at Colorado Springs. Between the stricken ground and the tormented sky we stood like lone survivors, feeling we had stepped off a back road into a war zone. It is in the back country that we look for restoration, and it is also in the back country that new death is being prepared.

Bruce
Berger

War of Curiosity

The mountains of the Gadsden Purchase country rise like islands from the Sonoran vegetation, archipelagos of ancient ranges the desert has buried and uncovered and buried again. Between them stretch the vast bajadas, inclined planes granulated from the mountains and tilted slightly toward each other so that the washes that swirl through them form vees in the central arroyo. A single jeep track often cuts through them like a demonstration of infinity. And every expanse leads back to the mountains so precisely inscribed on miniaturized horizons, the granitic ranges radiant with light, the volcanic ranges stopping it, blotting it out as if caught by imaginary clouds.

Remote, uncluttered, unreal: southwest Arizona is the perfect area for weapons testing. Twice during our week there we heard the tale of an Arizona state vehicle sent to help haul out a Wildlife Service helicopter that had crashed while making a survey of mountain sheep: the truck had been mistaken for one of the Air Force's immobile targets, and was strafed into oblivion while the two drivers fled in terror. We heard also of the droves of Mexicans crossing the same area, often carrying two gallon-sized milk cartons of water through thirty-five miles of total drought in the dead of summer; after the last picking season officials found a string of empty milk cartons and six bodies. And even newspapers carried the saga of the ongoing dope wars along the border, of federal agents unable to stanch the flow of narcotics to the north. Visited only by the social margins, nearly without water, reserved for the future of weaponry and the survival of endangered species, with consummate schizophrenia this waste lies on the final verge between life and death.

Having signed a document absolving the government from any responsibility for blowing us up, we crossed the bombing range and arrived at the wildlife refuge. We bounced slowly over the Camino del Diablo, the route pioneered by gold seekers and coast-bound travelers in the last century. We picked our way through great stone teeth scissored with faults, scrambled like brains, our boots slipping on the pinkish granite. We found strains of vegetation from Mexico—the gnarled turnip-like elephant trees, the rubber-producing guayule, the shrub called *sangre de drago:* dragon's blood. We drank from the few permanent springs and isolated pockets of water left by recent January storms. And everywhere we saw machine gun shells, small half-buried missiles that might have been still active, and drones—ten-foot wooden arrows that had been covered with cheap metal to simulate larger missiles, towed at supersonic speeds, fired at for one session, then cut from their cables to drop like paper airplanes into the ground, punctuating the distance with a strange upright glitter.

Bruce
Berger

On the fourth day we climbed a cinder cone so dark the saguaro stood luminous against it. Loaf-sized chunks of lava shone with maroon, ochre and raven, darkly iridescent, while between them grew minute winter flowers: tiny purple, tiny white. Scanning the far edge, a sawtooth range to the east fell northward to a horizon straight and clean as the sea, westward to a range wrinkled and withered as old insect life, past a scalloped horizon in Mexico and back full circle. The Camino del Diablo that brought us was blurred by vegetation, but Mexico's farther Highway 2 flashed with occasional trucks. Between those vague corridors filtered the jobless across a critical imaginary line.

From the cinder cone we threaded fields of lava to a clearing with a mano and metate intact, pottery sherds, shells that had apparently been traded from the gulf and bits of strewn quartz—whether of the ancient Cochise Culture, Hohokam or the more recent Sand Papago we didn't know. Over further stretches of lava we arrived at a playa, a valley bottom where water collected and left a large expanse of dust. And as we approached we saw unexpected life moving on the far side.

In so much waste we never thought to look for the Sonoran pronghorn, a species of antelope so rare there were perhaps sixty individuals left in the United States: yet here they were like a kind of grace. We crept cautiously forward and caught them in the field glasses. There was a group of four and another group of five. Suddenly the larger group appeared to sense us and started running—but what was this? They were running *toward* us. They hung in the binoculars, their feet a silent confusion pounding up dust as they grew larger, and at last filled our lenses near the playa's edge.

They were still perhaps two hundred feet off. Between us stood a haphazard row of creosote bushes. Stepping slowly, feet slightly preceding their torsos to minimize the sense of motion, a bold one lingering in the clearing, they advanced and stared until they were screened by the nearest foliage. We had ample time to take in their elegant light-colored bodies with the saddle marking, all eggshell and buff, their slender and graceful legs, their intimate heart-shaped faces with the small upthrust horns and large dark eyes. Something startled them, they dashed back across the playa nearly white from behind, paused while we scrambled closer to the creosote, then came back for another, more lingering look.

I thought fleetingly of the varieties of our kind their own had seen—Indians with their crude implements, padres, prospectors, immigrants, wildlife officials, adventurers, job seekers, hunters, dope runners. Even now the species that put them on the endangered list was preparing the MX missile over their heads, advancing its own status on the list. In such strange isolation each culture stood reduced to its consequences: what innocence was still possible? But mankind has all the historians, and the pronghorn lives, as we assume animals do, in the eternal moment. With a row of creosote bushes between us, ourselves at the edge of the desert, the pronghorn at the edge of the playa, we stood squared off and staring like opposing sides in a war of curiosity. And curiosity held us there in innocence, exploring with our eyes while our minds raced, sensing some secret in the other side worth getting to, before the pronghorn bolted once more and we turned back to our jeep. It is that attraction of creatures, not to be understood, that binds us to the future.

Bruce
Berger

As Above, So Below

Roads like beams of light aimed at the vanishing point, dots of vegetation so precise and alike they comprise an infinity of their own, far ranges in ethereal perspective: the desert is by nature unworldly. But this mountaintop is hived into domes, mounds, hemispheres, shafts, dormitories like so many skulled brains. And all of this complication, founded by the U. S. Government and a nonprofit corporation of thirteen universities, is trained on a responding void.

Since its first blast, the universe has expanded and progressively decanted itself, marking its chasms with dust clouds, galaxies, quasars and interstellar gases that are its peaks, oases and far valleys. It is entirely fitting that Kitt Peak, the world's largest collection of astronomical instruments, should command a raptor's view of the desert. The desert lover and the stargazer share the passion for distance, for the proximity of nonbeing that illumines what is. And in this little knot of brilliance, curiosity and postgraduate monomania a new spark is given off. It is here that absence maps itself. It is between voids that theories take shape. Looking down to the cactus, then up to the stars at the wild unlikelihood, one can affirm with Hermes Trismegistus, the medieval alchemist, his simple truism: as above, so below.

How to Look at a Desert Sunset

Too much has been made of desert sunsets, particularly in the captions of oversaturated magazine photos. Because desert skies tend to be clear, they can't match the Midwest for cloud effects or smog-inflamed cities for sheer longevity. But they are inferior only to novices who look, naively, in the direction of the setting sun, for the real desert sunset occurs in that unlikely direction, the east. It is opposite the sun that the last rays, deflected through clear skies, fall on the long, minutely-eroded mountain ranges and bathe our eyes with light of decreasing wavelengths and cooling colors— vermilion to salmon to plum—transporting the eastern horizon to islands of pure yearning.

Bruce Berger

The desert rat, so in love with distance that he commonly carries binoculars to bring it up close, instinctively focuses the dreamlike mountains to heighten the effect. Here an odd reversal takes place, for what is plum to the naked eye, confined and enlarged turns drab as cement, while the heaped knobs and extravagant spires turn out to be exfoliated granite. The observer knows how this stone weathers into rounded piles, how it crumbles underfoot, how it is colonized by black lichen. Fascinating as geology, it has been mastered by experience, turned to stone.

That is the revelation of desert sunsets: that the distance is so unmoored, so delicious, that you want to be there, to *become* that distance. And the closer you come—quickly, through binoculars, because it darkens even as you watch— the faster it burns into the ash of reality. Then you find out

that where you want to be is precisely where you began,
stripped to your bare eyes, watching as best you can,
yearning.

The
Telling
Distance

Among My Souvenirs

"Have you hiked across the island yet?" inquired the friendly middle-aged woman next to me at the campfire.

"This afternoon. I heard there was a dead whale to the north, so when I hit the Pacific I headed south."

"Not me," the woman replied. "Dead whales are my thing."

Bruce
Berger

I pressed for details. She had gotten ten fellow campers to help haul it above the tide line. She was excited: it was her first personal sei whale. She measured the skull, a whale's largest part, and worked out a plan. She could come back next month, get a boat to take it across Magdalena Bay, then hire a truck to haul it back up the Baja Peninsula to the border.

"You collect dead whales?" I murmured.

"If only my house were big enough! I do have a permit to take them across national borders, but the bulk of the whale goes to the county museum. The museum either keeps it or divvies it up to various specialists for study. I manage to keep some teeth, vertebrae, and baleen, and did have a wonderful vial of ambergris. I put a bit on my hands every morning, until the day my daughter-in-law told me she just threw out that little jar of stuff on my sink—whatever it was had gone real bad."

"Doesn't the whole whale smell real bad?"

"Not to me," she laughed. "My nose turns off after the first five minutes."

"Don't let her kid you," interjected her husband. "She

◆   222   ◆

doesn't even like a whale until the sun has turned it to Camembert."

Souvenirs are among the hazards of travel—even wilderness travel. As a child with frustrated wanderlust, when objects of nature and culture all ran together, I filled Chinese boxes with foreign stamps and coins, the odder the better. Sliding those panels reeking of cedar until they gave way to oval coins with square holes made my heart beat faster; postcards of undersea grottos, glaciers, or palmettos were portents of entire continents to be explored. But when I was old enough to collect those objects in person, I found them pale tokens of the lands they were supposed to represent. Postcards and trick boxes, it turned out, were sold to tourists like ourselves for our drab dollars, while coins and stamps were the local dimes and common postage. What reduced to commerce lost its appeal. Travel increasingly became a way to gather sensations, experiences, knowledge of new creatures—intangibles—and the only objects worth retrieving were the spoils of nature. Stones, feathers, sea horses, gourds, crystals, whales . . .

But even those purists who find, rather than buy, their mementos must face the question: what is so exquisite about proprietorship that we will haul home, on beachwalks or backpacks, what might be photographed, celebrated in a journal, shared with friends on the spot, and left for the next arrival? Why must nature's accretions be wrenched from their sockets? Why do we risk spinal dislocation for what looks on the windowsill like detritus?

First it must be noted that no one who harvests lavender rocks, hawk feathers, or fox skulls is concerned with the representative, or with merely proving he has been there. Collectors' eyes have a narrowed, predatory focus, and from miles of flung sand they pry out the chambered nautilus. The French poet Valéry imagines a man without previous knowledge of seashells discovering a calcareous tube coiling inward in regularly diminishing partitions. Would he really guess it was secreted by blind instinct, or would he assume a conscious artisan? Whatever he concludes, if he is a collector he will pick it up. And here we reach the central irony—which is that natural objects we favor have a human, even superhuman, degree of articulation, hue, and expressiveness. From all our globe engenders we select the most complex, the most structured, the most highly colored: the most similar to creations of our dominant kind. It is as if matter had been deliberately organized to evoke a journey in one's life, an episode which is itself a crystal amid the slag of routine. Collecting is most unnatural selection.

The fusion of the civilized and the wild infects all of nature's pickpockets, even the scientist on duty. Objects taken for their design touch whatever sensibility responds to painting and sculpture, while those that play on household objects become paperweights, soap dishes, door stops, and hat racks. Sticks and odd rocks that mimic other objects of nature, manufactured goods, or one's fellow human beings often turn into private jokes, a kind of found caricature. A friend of mine takes baths with a pet rock shaped like a waterbug, while another makes mobiles of driftwood that resembles bits of human anatomy. Objects are conscripted for works of art to be assembled at home by the collector, or to fill gaps in a series and satisfy the collector's urge to completeness. Even the detached scientist is motivated by his curiosity, or his contract. No matter how purely one approaches natural souvenirs, it is hard to stray from the human bias.

A case worth examining, since it brings into play the natural, the manufactured, and the raid on our heritage, is the rage for arrowheads. Otherwise amusing desert rats will wander heads-down in circles for long dusty hours while companions make cracks about the agate and the ecstasy. Why? In the well-turned arrow, they argue, craftsman and stone reach idyllic fusion. One imagines the mental state of the shaper: was he considering beauty as

Bruce Berger

well as utility? Calmly looking forward to the hunt? Staring starvation in the face? The artifact is a bridge between our own physical comfort and a time not far behind us when existence was won from day to day. Opulent geology beaten into weapons, then turned by time into jewels, has been further transformed by collectors into fetishes.

A man from Genoa once told me he collected hyena dung that had been struck by lightning. While never invited to contemplate *that* collection, I have often wondered since whether chemistry and chance have come up with such a substance, and have brooded at length over a piece of coprolite I paid a quarter for at a park-and-swap in a small town in Arizona. Coprolite, I have learned, is mineralized feces, and this example was executed by a turtle that lived in an inland sea where the park-and-swap now stood. How big was the turtle? What did it eat? Is this relic of one meal the single piece of him that remains undispersed? How long before the invention of money, for which I exchanged his keepsake, did he produce it? By what evolutionary process do we, a later species, offer it for barter? Is money our own excreta? Exactly what kind of universe *is* this?

Acquisition as a branch of philosophy? I glance at my own shelf with its river rocks from Glen Canyon. From the miniature tugboat to the acne specimen they flash with color, sometimes parody objects they are not, and principally they memorialize for me a spot now silting up under the wastes of Lake Powell. Like Ming vases to an Orientalist, they recall a high and vanished civilization. For others it is the Anasazi culture evoked through a chalcedony bird point, or the high civilization of whales, loved enough to haul home the entire creature as token of itself. Geodes, seed pods, pelican beaks, cholla skeletons, limestone accretions, shed snakeskins, even fossil dung, arrayed on our sills, allow our imaginations to keep traveling while the rest of us stays still.

Collectors are more than usually sensitive to the world's

The Telling Distance

225

sheer abundance, but to enjoy it they must narrow it down. The crosscurrents of our biosphere are too complex to take in, and we are as naive as the beachwalker who happens upon a shell with its precisely enfolded scroll and finds it emblematic of a universe working itself out in an unknown direction, with staggering precision. For many of us the traditional answers are too simple, or even insulting, and the scientific answers are incomprehensible. The world we live in, meanwhile, is increasingly artificial and oppressive. In such a Babel we pick up the shell, perhaps, because for those of us obsessed with our surroundings it comes closer than the saint or the formula to an image we can care for. Set up in our homes as icons once were, our natural souvenirs testify to a continuing belief in order, significance, and beauty: what was once called awe. Whatever we finally conclude about the world, we still admire it enough to try, vainly and in bits, to keep it.

Bruce
Berger

The San Rafael Swell Motel

Lying one day's drive from the Escalante River, the Maze and several other prime locations, the wash was for years a convenient overnight car camp. A string of cottonwoods, spaced like bad teeth, formed a quarter-mile crescent through which a streambed wound back and forth frosted with alkali. Across the western horizon spread the crimson and taffy spires, domes, upheavals and twists of a fault called the San Rafael Swell, and to the south sat a rock like a vermilion temple. At either end the wash trailed into barrenness lost among low hills. Offering the only foliage for miles around, scattered with the tracks, hoofprints and tire treads of creatures never seen, with a few birds phrasing the silence and the sense of an arthritic hand exhausted from squeezing the sky, this way-station haunted me long after our glamorous destinations.

Recent migrations had led me elsewhere, I hadn't been back for a half dozen years, and I had almost forgotten the turn-off. But as soon as we rounded the crest and I saw the mangy trees still rattling their green, my heart began to pound. It was nearing sundown and the San Rafael Swell strode forward, deep-shadowed and incandescent. My friends grabbed their cooking equipment and sleeping bags. I grabbed a beer from the cooler and wandered off for a private reunion.

The very grains of alkali seemed unchanged. As I reached the bend, five barn owls wheeled just overhead, pale and silent, each disk-like face peering for an instant into mine with small black eyes. A single pool mirrored the great rock turning slowly to blood. Insects sounded the bass note of being. I inspected the wash later by flashlight, and again, coffee cup in hand, the next morning. Then, as usual, we were off.

Someday the wash will be my destination. I will stay a few days. I will hike the streambed in both directions and discover what it does in the low hills. I will sit with binoculars and patience, deciphering the animals, learning the birds. I will feel the extremes of temperature, the range of light. Or maybe I will always touch and go, leaving the wash half-dreamt with its scraggy trees, its shadows of hoofs, scales and claws, its singing finches and bees, its single pools, the vortex of desolation and center of a universe: mine.

Bruce
Berger

Fernando and Marisela

The drawers of nightstands are filled with hexes against the long dark—a small cross, a book of sayings, a bottle of Valium. For reasons unclear to me, I keep a piece of litter I found under a cactus outside Tucson. I was staying in one of those transition zones where fresh houses breach the desert. My hostess was the developer, a woman who built custom homes—living in one while she supervised the next—until she had designed and inhabited all the houses on a little lane named for herself. It was June, 1974, and the temperature was 115. Bored with the air conditioning, stunned outside, I wandered between the lady's constructions poking at the small.

Otherwise I never would have spotted a scrap so bland and so dense. I reached carefully between the barbs of fallen cholla, tweezering it out between thumb and forefinger. I unfolded it once, then again. An inch and a half square unfurled, it was a portrait of a girl against a neutral backdrop, snapped in a cheap studio or perhaps a machine. In her late teens, with full but sad features, she gazed into the lens with moist dark eyes, black lashes, black eyebrows, and dyed blond hair. Though the photo was in black and white, you could tell she had one of those bleach jobs that turns dark hair reddish and leaves it murky at the roots. On the other side, in schoolgirl cursive, she had written in Spanish, "Fernando, though you are far away, don't feel alone, for there is one who remembers and will wait for you always. Marisela, Nogales, Sonora. April 17, 1972."

The desert is known for keeping the most fragile objects intact for years. Dated two years back, the photo might have spent its life under the cholla. But two seasons of winter drizzle and two of summer thundershowers had not turned the paper brittle, nor had two years of burning sun yellowed a corner of the back. The photograph, so charged with unknown lives, had barely preceded me.

But had it been lost or thrown away? The photo gallery in one's pocket seems one more tense of a Spanish verb, and Latin wallets resemble souvenir albums with money in the binding. Marisela's snapshot would have fit neatly in a plastic leaf, and perhaps it had. Yet it had been doubled and quartered so that her face was disfigured by the crosshairs of folds as if by a rifle sight, leaving the tiny quadrangle more unwieldy than before. Marisela hadn't been lost; she had been freshly and consciously discarded.

Bruce Berger

Though you are far away . . . Were all of Marisela's friends dyeing their hair that year, or did she do it just for Fernando? She presumably gave him her picture before he headed to find work in a land where the girls were blonde and radiant. When he was far away, surrounded by golden Americans, the photo would remind him that he had a blonde girlfriend back home. The Yankified glamor falsified Marisela's own beauty, but her dewy black eyes held their ground with perfect honesty, perfect desperation.

Far away . . . Yet Tucson is not far; it is a quick and cheap bus ride back to Nogales, a day's excursion. Did Fernando go back to see Marisela? Surely at first. But two years is a long time for a young man tasting the novelties of another country. If she tried to hold him with those pleading moist eyes, he would only have felt trapped and resentful, less inclined to bus himself into the past. If he showed up less often, she would turn icy, then accusative. He might easily drop out of her life, not even think of her for months. One hot spring day, working construction for a lady who built custom homes, he weeded through his wallet during a cigarette break, and ran across this embarrassing back number, this phony blonde who was two years and one language late. Perhaps there was a quick stab of regret, but you couldn't be sentimental forever.

Marisela, it is over a decade since a passing gringo, stunned by the heat, rescued your photo from beneath a cactus. You were right to let your hair grow dark, to embark on adulthood, to forget the worthless Fernando. After high school your friends married and began families, or became shopgirls, or sold themselves in the streets to Fernando's new cronies from across the border. Nogales is not a town where jilted girlfriends pine by the casement, nor were you the Lady of Shalott. Fernando has doubtless pursued the construction dollar and begun a family with another person, probably not blonde. He no longer works for the lady who built custom homes, for she has died, the cactus she left between her constructions has filled with other homes, and her name is kept fresh only by a street sign. The desert is less and less able to keep what we throw away, and your photo barely preceded the bulldozer.

But if you ever feel alone in your new life as a mother, a salesperson, a streetwalker, remember that there is someone far north of Nogales, far north of Tucson, who is unaccountably haunted by your eyes, and who keeps your photograph within reach for solace in the night.

The Telling Distance

Desert Moon Hotel Revisited

Bruce
Berger

As I'd foreseen, it was years before I bothered to take the Thompson exit on Interstate 70 and check up on the Desert Moon Hotel. The pavement still wound a thin mile to Thompson's crumbling main street—once, unbelievably, a commercial stretch on a coast-to-coast artery. The little railroad station sported a shiny Amtrak sign, and the three vague blocks retained their assortment of odd buildings. The buildings, in fact, were odder than I'd remembered, and I parked in front of a freshly painted art deco affair that escaped me entirely. A design on the side wall showed yellow liquid spilling from a test tube onto a globe, beside which ran, in vertical caps, the word HEMOTECHNICS. Aggressive lettering at the far end of the facade—Shipping, Restricted Entry, Authorized Personnel Only—surrounded a metal door that appeared to have been blasted open. Across the street, one side of the sign of the inoperative Thompson Motel had been covered by a larger sign that read, "Zone, Inc." Or if the globe before "Zone" was meant for a letter, the concern was "Ozone, Inc." A building on the corner radiated bright discordant colors. All I could surmise was that Thompson, bypassed by the interstate, was being revived by schismatics from the solar industry.

But on to my destination. I walked a block west to the Desert Moon Hotel, still dingy white, still sporting its sign with a winking moon. Through a side door screen I could see someone stirring in the kitchen but I thought I should approach properly, through the front door. It was locked. I returned to the side door. Soon a seventyish man came out and asked, in a pleasant voice, my business.

"Do you have a room for the night?"

He laughed. "This place hasn't been open for ten years. In fact for three years there was nobody here at all, but last year we moved back and decided to make a house out of it."

"Doesn't seem that long. One night I stayed in that room," I said, pointing to the upstairs window in the right corner.

"You did? Why?"

"Needed a place for the night," I lied, having come purely out of curiosity.

"The roof leaks in that room now, and the whole upstairs plumbing is shot. But, do you know, when my daddy built this place in 1934 it was the hottest thing on the highway. We three kids pumped the gas, and we sold more gallons than we do out on the interstate now."

"What's happening over there?" I asked, pointing to the freshly painted buildings. "Some kind of solar energy?"

"Lot dumber than that. In fact it's the dumbest thing I've ever heard of. It's a film set. Supposed to be a comedy about good spirits and bad spirits, called *Sundown Vampires in Retreat*. They painted a bunch of buildings in town and, wouldn't you know, the only one of mine they painted is the one I'm tearing down next year. In fact the only thing they really left is that," he concluded, pointing to a tawny mound in the street. "Manure."

I walked past my car, to the service entrance of HEMOTECHNICS. On closer inspection the explosion was crafted by sheared sheet metal. I stepped through it and found myself still outside, facing the railroad tracks and, beyond, the batwing sprawl of Book Cliffs. This wasn't even a tricked-out old building; it was a two-sided false front. Its sole piece of furniture was a makeshift table holding a pop bottle full of brads. I sat on the ground, leaned against a wall support, and tried to imagine what, if anything, these developments meant. *New uses for old arteries* is what surfaced instead of insight. Suddenly a roar came from the east, and a lonely blaring horn. A man waved to me from the engine, perhaps taking me for a good vampire. He was followed by fifty-seven cars, slatted cars full of tiny white hatchbacks, empty boxcars, high-domed cars whose contents remained mysterious. Dust settled, then silence. I turned rigid when the building itself made hollow battering noises straight over my head. I stood up and peered. It was months after nesting season, but sparrows were frantically engaged in organized activity in a hollow above a cross-beam. They had eye stripes and pinkish bills, but the bird book I keep in the car didn't show anything quite like them.

So Thompson, bypassed so many years by the interstate, was newly undead—and I let only two months pass before I next revisited. I coasted to the stop sign, intending to take in the art deco sweep of HEMOTECHNICS, to find myself staring straight through to the eroding bats of Book Cliffs. Both facades had vanished. The Zone, Inc. sign was down from the inoperative Thompson Motel, and the street was clean of manure. It was as if the designed and carpentered solids of movie sets were as fleeting as the arrangements of light they served.

I parked under the Amtrak sign and walked the tracks, then back on the main street past the Desert Moon Hotel. I scoured the corner lot for any vestige of HEMOTECHNICS. All I found, beside blown packaging from distant fast food outlets, were bits of a turquoise material I couldn't quite identify but that seemed vaguely plastic and may have formed part of the art deco trim. It was the same color that Everett Ruess, scorner of jewelry, wore on his wrist because it reminded him of "a bit of sky." Where, in that sky, were the unidentifiable sparrows that sought out-of-season nesting in a fictitious concern called HEMOTECHNICS? To broaden the question, why do mirages recede at every approach?

Bruce Berger

◆ *234* ◆

The Christmas Agave

The last day of November dawned luminous as stained glass. A brisk wind had polished the sky, a low sun turned the mountains luminous blue, and sycamores rattled like parchment in the arroyos. Even in the desert such splendor cannot last; clearly it was time to gather the Christmas agave.

I drove from Phoenix out past the Fort McDowell Reservation, pondering the ethics of agave-cutting. Also called a century plant, the agave lives a quarter of a century, sends up a stalk, blooms and dies. By now the seeds would have scattered; the cycle would be complete. By robbing the desert of one shaft of pulp I would be sparing a young pine. Feeling a little guilty to be armed with a yardstick and hacksaw, my environmental conscience was nonetheless appeased, even a little flushed.

The highway itself had autumnal compensations: the catclaw touched with saffron, the rabbit brush cloudy with seeds, some anonymous ground weed turning the runoff to pools of russet and gold. I turned off toward Four Peaks and clattered up the dirt tracks, keeping an eye out for all yuccas and agaves. The first species was a small yucca with no stems at all, then after several miles a related species appeared bearing a single branchless feathery shaft: sotol, spectacular but useless for the purpose. Up through the life zones, the cactus thinning, the scrub massing its small leathery leaves, condensing to chaparral, the homogeneous green now broken only by leafless black mesquite. My mind wandered, my eyes drifted toward the far blue, and suddenly the teeth of Four Peaks were skewered with the very shape I was after.

I pulled off the road and bailed out. Along the roadside ran a small arroyo, then a hillside with a healthy stand of *Agave parryi*. Yardstick and saw in hand, I crashed through a tangle of mountain mahogany, then scrambled a steep hillside. Agave stalks rose from rosettes of dead spikes, branching into panicles of burst pods like handfuls of wooden flowers. Less monumental than the grandest of century plants, it was all that would fit in my jeep. The lowest branches sprouted two thirds of the way up the stalk, spacing themselves eight inches apart to a bunched crown; I would be culling, so to speak, the tip of the asparagus.

I cased the hillside, then selected the most symmetrical and generous of limb. I pulled the trunk toward me and the root system tore easily from the ground, tumbling the stalk like a dancer into my hands. I suspended it between a couple of boulders, measured it and found myself in luck: from tip to just below the bottom branch was eight feet— precisely the interior diagonal of my jeep. The stem sawed cleanly, and with little effort I carried aloft this elegant tree half again my height over thickets of bayberry and mountain mahogany. Barely touching the far corners of my jeep, crowding my shift arm, it rode in state as I crouched under its pods and bounced gingerly back to Phoenix.

After Christmases of wrestling with sticky spruce and unwieldy hemlock, it was a joy simply to stick an agave in the stand and twist the screws. It stood far leaner, more spare than the traditional tree. With the branch tips already thick with pods, we were able to fit less than half of the usual clutter. By necessity we clustered it around the pods—golden balls, silver birds and flying fish, and two strings of tiny white lights wound in delicate spirals to a small Pleiades on top. Less traditional ornaments included a green plastic tag with the number 173—once a cow's pierced earring—and twists of lavender, cream and blaze

Bruce
Berger

orange surveyor's tape unlittered from public lands. Even these were deployed with taste and the total effect was airy and precise, the inflection of a Balinese dancer. Standing by the front window, it let the sun flood through undimmed by day, and by night afforded Roosevelt St. a restful constellation of tiny stars.

Like any innovation, it had its detractors. There were the wits who called it yucca with an unfortunate stress on the first syllable, and one who pitied our poor tree for losing all its needles. Someone informed me that while agave-culling might be environmentally sound, it was illegal without a permit, and second cousin to cactus-rustling. But Garret wanted a Christmas agave of his own, Cat Martha wanted one for her twelve cats, and loose talk surfaced about leaving it up all year.

And what began admittedly in jest surprised us with meaning. The traditional tannenbaum, with its origin in the mists of Bavaria, has become progressively tricked out with lights, emblazoned in chains and baubles, crusted with artificial snow, bloated and embalmed in spangles, plastic icicles and tinsel. Lately its very shape has been mocked by erector set aluminum and by obelisks of sprayed petroleum products. Heaped with the excreta of free enterprise, flashing like Las Vegas, a shrine to glut, if the contemporary Christmas tree has a Biblical allusion left, it is the Whore of Babylon.

When a tradition exhausts itself in decadence, it is time to look elsewhere. If only by contrast, and by accident, the Christmas agave suggested something of the restraint, the gift of unmateriality, the metaphysical elegance that was reportedly born on Christmas Day.

The original Holy Land was, after all, a desert.

The Telling Distance

Postlude

Walking into the Future

It is generally conceded that for the wilderness traveler the real fall of man was the industrial revolution. The machine, that bitten apple, has blown life's flow into shrapnel, bombarding the ear and eye, parching the tongue, leaving touch and smell to wither and die. Now it threatens our very survival. And behind the machine, its demonic spirit, is corporate enterprise with its brutalizing competition, its deadlines and discontinuities, its official lies, computerizing our secrets and revising our lives. Wilderness, loved for its own sake, has increasingly become a place to escape the industrial web, to scrape off our century, to prepare an inner clearing for one's spirit and one's biological rhythms.

Yet consider our contemporary on the brink of a trip. He takes out a backpack weighing two to five pounds, a nylon configuration of compartments and pockets on an aluminum frame. Into it go his white gas or butane burner, his aluminum pot nest, and a utensil set that clamps to the bulk of four pencils. Next come his sleeping bag, four to six pounds and toasty to zero or forty below, a foam pad, then a parka that wads into a stuff bag the size of a cantaloupe. For sustenance there is dehydrated linguine, beef almondine, noodles Romanoff, shrimp creole and French apple compote. There are elegant options like folding lanterns with mica windows, insect repellent hankies, collapsible scissors, portable pressure cookers, nylon hammocks and esoterica from Dr. Scholl, as well as regulation cameras, binoculars and notebooks. All of this is available, if not at bargain rates, at the sports emporia that grace our jumping-off points.

Consider as well the cultural preparations. The average backpacker has absorbed through his American skin a constellation of attitudes on self-reliance and the exaltation of nature from Emerson, Thoreau, Muir and Burroughs. He is aware that everything is hitched to everything else and that one should think like a mountain, and has delved, if literary, into Rachel Carson, Aldo Leopold, Loren Eiseley, Edward Abbey and Annie Dillard. He is provisioned with contour maps like fingerprints of the beyond, pocket guides to the area, skeleton keys to the flora and fauna. In flight from contemporary civilization, he conscripts every convenient product in pursuing the alternative.

Bruce
Berger

"Every revolution is part revival," says Philip Slater in *The Pursuit of Loneliness*, and the camping revolution is no exception. Half glimpsed in the current rush to the wilds, the romantic myth at its core, is the dream of a lost paradise: for an American, the time of the pioneer. Subject to local variation, the vision shimmers from a time before Edison and Henry Ford, before bulldozers and chain saws, when even businessmen and politicians were at the mercy of the weather. Crops were planted by phases of a moon not yet eclipsed by arc lamps. The hearth blazed with trees one could name. The dark was honed by owls and coyotes, not traffic and television. Horizons were clear, air waves were audible without a transmitter, and the joy of spring was no metaphor. Endurance was a deep congruence between natural and human seasons.

The myth of the pioneer is powerful, even inevitable, but let us glance at the pioneer himself. On the brink of his own expedition he hefts his blankets, his bags of flour, his woolen clothing, his iron skillet and his shooting iron into his saddlebags, with perhaps a pack animal or even a wagon to haul it all. His preparation is unassisted by specialty shops. His motive for braving the unknown is to get across it, trap it, map it, mine it, homestead it, perhaps to get rich on it. The chance he is out for knowledge, transcendental experience or artistic raw material, not unknown, is remote, and vacation for him is the time he spends back home. He has his own myths, but they are likely to revolve around survival, rectitude and material gain.

The backpacker as mythologist, then, lacks credibility. But all humanity needs some sort of internal prop, however artificial, to keep from going over the edge. Perhaps what today's walker needs is something more contemporary, more image-building, which will find him on the cutting edge of history rather than choking in its wake. This might be accomplished by the simple expedient of turning him 180 degrees around so that he faces, instead of the benighted pioneer, someone at the very forefront of our time. Like the backpacker, this figure is a romantic: not out for material gain—not yet anyway—but to find out what's there. He carries with him a portable defense against inclement events. His back-up systems have been prepared in advance. He takes careful pictures, brings back souvenirs, keeps records for the folks back home. He cooks by pouring hot water into a pouch, munches space sticks and guzzles Tang, and he is out there prowling the verge.

Certain hardliners will argue, no doubt, that the abyss between the backpacker and the astronaut makes identification impractical. The backpacker requires no vast ground crew, no instruction from mission control. His every move is not subject to calculation and electrical monitoring. His portable life-support system is not a straight jacket. He needn't suck existence through a tube. He is not prevented from skinny-dipping.

But however much the backpacker may emulate the pioneer, he is by heritage the pioneer's opposite, and however much he may scorn the industrial revolution, he is vastly in its debt. As if under a Taiwanese wand, camping equipment is miniaturized, streamlined, sophisticated, drained of weight and bulk. Its hardware is metal or plastic or polymorphic, ingenious, adaptable to shifting circumstance. Its software is airy, insulating, collapsible and chic. Meticulously organized, the flower of complex and collective thought, the loaded pack—like the space module—is fully a vehicle of our century's last quarter, and sits squarely on contemporary shoulders.

The time has come for the backpacker to accept his role and embrace his own revolution, for it is he who has democratized the space program. While the astronaut focuses the yearning of cramped humanity on a shrinking planet, it is the backpacker who acts out that aspiration, who eliminates the star system and lowers the cost until it is often cheaper than staying put. Once he has struck out he is free of home gravity. His machine is on his back; he can go where his footsteps decide. His social relations, like those of the astronauts, are channeled toward cooperation rather than aggression. He is not out for pelts, land grants or a hot riff on his Geiger counter; he is more interested in life as he doesn't know it—new plants, strange rocks, unknown fauna, bones, scat, bogs, space, light, peace. Technological breakthroughs lighten his feet while his pores let the universe in. A walk into the wilderness, at the close of the twentieth century, is a space walk.

It is no accident that the famous view of the earth from the moon, frequently cited as one justification for the entire space program, has supplanted the flag and the cross as a mobilizing symbol for a new generation. With a space traveler's awareness of what is unique within a few light years, ours is the fight to salvage the web that produced, with all its props and absurdities, the human mind. Often the wilderness vanguard—aping styles of the sixties, playing eco-saboteur, clowning to the popular nostalgia—seems a self-mocking sideshow. But every civilization, culturally as well as genetically, must preserve multiplicity

Bruce
Berger

to survive, and what seems a throwback may be the variation selected to lead the way out. The technician, the industrialist and the revolutionary are having their day. The ultimate function of myth, however, is not to interpret reality but to create it. Perhaps if we hold on for a bit longer, survival in the post-industrial age—if industry allows survival at all—may find the earthbound trail walker buckling on his trackless helium shoes and hoisting his aerodynamic non-gravitational pack, to take civilization's next step.

The
Telling
Distance